# Sower's Seeds That Nurture Family Values
## Sixth Planting

by

## Brian Cavanaugh, T.O.R.

**Paulist Press**
New York    Mahwah, N.J.

*Also by Brian Cavanaugh, T.O.R.*
*Published by Paulist Press*

THE SOWER'S SEEDS
MORE SOWER'S SEEDS: SECOND PLANTING
FRESH PACKET OF SOWER'S SEEDS: THIRD PLANTING
SOWER'S SEEDS APLENTY: FOURTH PLANTING
SOWER'S SEEDS OF VIRTUE (SPIRITUAL SAMPLER)
SOWER'S SEEDS OF ENCOURAGEMENT: FIFTH PLANTING

*Cover design by Nicholas T. Markell; cover illustration inspired by Fran Balles Goodman*

Library of Congress Cataloging-in-Publication Data

Sower's seeds that nurture family values : sixth planting / [edited] by Brian Cavanaugh.
    p.  cm.
  Includes bibliographical references and index.
  ISBN 0-8091-3938-3 (alk. paper)
  1. Homiletical illustrations. 2. Family—Religious life. 3. Catholic preaching. I. Cavanaugh, Brian, 1947-
BV4225.2.C39 2000
251'.08—dc21

                                        00-021473

Published by Paulist Press
997 Macarthur Boulevard
Mahwah, New Jersey 07430

www.paulistpress.com

Printed and bound in the
United States of America

# Contents

# Dedication

This sixth book in the Sower's Seeds series, *Sower's Seeds That Nurture Family Values,* is dedicated to my sisters, Barbara and Maureen, to my brother, Michael, and to their families for inviting me into their lives and sharing in their family experiences.

# Acknowledgments

Can you believe it! It is ten years since the first book in the Sower's Seeds series was published. That these books are sold worldwide still amazes me. It is a thrill to talk with someone, or receive a message from someone, who says that they saw my books in a bookstore in Rome, in Dublin, in Trinidad, or in Australia. I hope I never get so jaded that such a message is no longer exciting. I thank you all who now share in the sowing of these seeds. Plant them well, and water often. Enjoy!

My sincerest gratitude is saved for both of my editors: Donna Menis, a valued colleague, friend and, most of all, source of encouragement and support. Donna, thank you for your superb editorial insights, criticisms and suggestions.

Also, a special thank you to Paulist Press for the wisdom in allowing me to collaborate with such a gifted editor as Maria Maggi. Maria, thank you for suggesting this special collection of stories that hopefully addresses some of the special needs that are facing families today.

# Introduction
## Become Beacons of Light

The idea for an introduction to this book on family values first developed during my preparation of a homily to commemorate the forty-eighth National Day of Prayer, which occurs annually on the first Thursday of May. During this preparation, my thoughts were still reeling, like aftershocks, from the tragic school shootings in Littleton, Colorado, and memories were stirred of similar events in Paducah, Kentucky, and Jonesborough, Arkansas. I wondered what has happened in today's society so that children killing children has replaced the schoolyard fights with a bully that I remember. Today, is there a message of hope that we can give to our families, our communities, our nation, our world?

The books in this Sower's Seeds series are my simple attempts to sow a few "seeds" of hope, inspiration and encouragement in a world that seems so desperate to hear an uplifting word. With that in mind, I share with you some of my thoughts from that forty-eighth National Day of Prayer homily.

The National Day of Prayer Task Force distributed a flyer presenting the 1999 theme: *Light the Nation...with prayer.* The Task Force also suggested that Matthew 5:13–16 be read, with emphasis on:

> *You are the light of the world....Just so, your light must shine before others, that they may see your good deeds and glorify your heavenly Father.* (vv. 14, 16 NAB)

As a nation, a community and a family, we are presented with a serious challenge that we must face. The Task Force

1

notes, "…if the world is becoming darker, the problem is not with the darkness. The problem is with the light." It continues, "As an earthly tabernacle of God's love, you are to be a refuge that attracts the needy; a central point to which those from all walks of life can receive comfort, sustenance and protection as you point them to the all-powerful Savior.…Because of Christ's radiance within you, people and situations surrounding you should be changing for the better."

Simply put, we need to join together and become beacons of light in a world that seemingly is growing ever darker and colder. Now it may come as a shock to some of you folks, but in my line of work I've done a fair amount of lighting candles. In so doing, I discovered an illuminating spark of wisdom that I want to share with you. It is this—if one candle will take of its own warmth, brilliance and power and share of itself to light another, it loses nothing. It multiplies itself. Now, if these two candles take of their own warmth, brilliance and power and share of themselves to light another, they lose nothing. They have multiplied themselves—all in geometric proportions: 2-4-8-16-32, and so on.

You see, each of us needs to become a *candlelighter!* It was President Abraham Lincoln who once said, "I am not bound to win, but I am bound to be true. I am not bound to succeed but I am bound to live up to what light I have." Actually, that's all that is expected from each one of us: *to live up to what light I have.*

Yet, there is a daily struggle with duality in life, of which the Star Wars movies forcefully remind us. There is Yin and Yang, angels and devils, and two sides to the Force—Light and Dark. Thus, there are both *candlelighters* and *candlesnuffers*. The latter think that if they can snuff out someone else's candle, it will make theirs seem brighter. However all they really do is make this world a little bit darker and a whole lot colder. Remember, "*You* are the light of the world." And now is the time to take up the challenge and become *candlelighters*. It is the time for you to become beacons of light!

2

"Be a Lamplighter," a story from my third book, *Fresh Packet of Sower's Seeds,* might illuminate this point.

Several parents were sitting on a neighbor's porch discussing their children. They were talking about the negative environment in which the kids had to grow up—an environment filled with drugs, violence and a pervading feeling of hopelessness. How could they, the parents, bring any light into their children's world since it seemed so dark and hopeless? Could they be enough of a positive influence in their children's lives that the children would not just survive, but possibly work to change the world around them? The discussion went on for some time.

One of the parents, a science teacher, remarked, "I think we can make a difference in our children's lives if we become lamplighters."

"Lamplighters? What do you mean?" the others asked.

She explained. "Around the turn of the century a lamplighter went around the streets lighting the street lamps. He carried a long pole that had a small candle on top with which he would reach up to light the kerosene-fed lamps," she said. "But from a distance you could not see a lamplighter very well. The light from one small candle was not very bright in the surrounding darkness of night."

"However," she continued, "you could follow the progress of the lamplighter as he went along a street. The presence of his candle was barely visible until it joined with the flame of the street lamp being newly lit. A radiant glow erased a portion of the night's darkness and, looking back down the street, you could see that the light from the glowing street lamps made the entire street bright as day. The darkness was held at bay."

Almost as a chorus the parents exclaimed, "That's it! We'll be lamplighters for our children. We'll be their role models. We'll share from our own flame in order to light each child's individual lamp of wisdom and by our love provide the fuel necessary to nourish and sustain its flame. Then we will have helped them become bright enough themselves so that they can conquer the darkness and hopelessness of their world."

This story wonderfully illustrates the wisdom of Pope John XXIII, who once said, "Every believer in this world must become a spark of light." Likewise, the National Day of Prayer Task Force exhorts us, individually and collectively, to remember that it is the radiance of Christ within you that helps the people and situations you touch change for the better. As your actions confirm the gospel message that "You are the light of the world," may others "see your good deeds and glorify your heavenly Father" (Mt 5:14, 16 NAB).

**In Our Home...**
(adapted from
1 Thes 5:11, 13, 15–18)

Brian Cavanaugh, T.O.R.

In our Home…
We encourage one another,
We build one another up,
We are at peace with each other,
We seek to do good,
We rejoice,
We give thanks,
We pray constantly,
In our Home.

# 1.
## Given Up Hope Until...

### Anonymous

A pastor tells of the experience of a young woman at a local children's hospital. She was asked by a teacher from her church to tutor a boy with some schoolwork while he was in the hospital. The woman didn't realize until she got to the hospital that the boy was in the burn unit, in considerable pain and barely able to respond. She tried to tutor him, stumbling through the English lesson, ashamed at putting him through such a senseless exercise.

The next day, when she returned to the hospital, a nurse asked her, "What did you do to that boy?" Before she could finish apologizing, the nurse interrupted her: "You don't understand. His entire attitude has changed. It's as though he has decided to live!"

A few weeks later, the boy explained that he had completely given up hope until this young woman arrived. With joyful tears he explained, "They wouldn't send a tutor to work on nouns and verbs with a dying boy, would they?"

Sometimes we are invited into people's lives and into places and events that, on the surface, have no meaning or purpose to us. We ask ourselves, what are we doing here? What purpose do we have here? Often we define our lives only by what we can see or understand; we forget that we are a part of something larger than ourselves. When we forget, we miss opportunity after opportunity, those moments of grace, to affect our world for the better.

# 2.
# The Noblest Solution

## Anonymous

A man built a prosperous business through zealous toil and honest dealings. As he advanced in age, he felt concerned about the future of his enterprise because he had no children or close relatives, except for three nephews.

One day he summoned the young men and declared, "I have a problem, and whoever comes up with the best solution will inherit all that I possess."

Giving each of them an equal amount of money, he instructed them to buy something that would fill his large office. "Spend no more than I have given you," he directed, "and be sure you are back by sunset."

All day long each nephew attempted separately to fulfill his uncle's instructions. Finally, when the shadows lengthened, they obediently returned to make their report. Their uncle awaited them, anxious to see their purchases.

The first nephew dragged in a few huge sacks of Styrofoam® packing "peanuts" that nearly filled the office when the sacks were emptied. After the room was cleared, the second nephew brought in bundles and bundles of helium-filled balloons that floated throughout the office, filling it better than the Styrofoam®. The third nephew stood silent and forlorn. His uncle inquired of him, "So what have you to offer?"

"Uncle," replied the nephew, "I spent half of my money to help a family whose house burned down last night. Then I ran into some kids in trouble and gave most of the rest to an inner-city youth center. With the little bit I had left, I bought this candle and matches." Then he lit the candle and its glowing light filled every corner of the room!

The kindly old uncle realized that here was the noblest of his family. He blessed the nephew for making the best use of his gift and welcomed him into his business.

# 3.
## To Have a Great Theme
### (adapted)

## Harry Huxhold

A great writer once said that a great book requires a great theme. So does a great life. An endless stream of books are meaningless and will not last as great literature because they do not have a great theme.

So it is with people. All too much in human history is wasted and meaningless because there is no great theme, no great purpose in life.

Men and women have a deep hunger in life for meaning and purpose, but so often they are afraid to let go of a self-centered ego. To have a great theme in life involves taking the risk of moving beyond the narrow limitations of "me" and discovering one's true self where Jesus is at the center—nurturing, healing and empowering us to be men and women for others. Here is our great theme, our meaning and purpose.

# 4.
## The Trouble Tree

## Anonymous

There was a carpenter who just finished a rough day on the job. A flat tire made him lose an hour of work, his electric saw quit working and now his ancient pickup truck refused to start. While his foreman drove him home, he fumed in stony silence. Arriving at his home, he invited his boss to meet his family. As they walked toward the house, the carpenter paused briefly at a large pine tree, touching the tips of the branches with both hands.

When he opened the front door, he underwent an amazing transformation. His tanned face glowed with smiles and hugs for his two small children; then he gave a long embrace and kiss to his wife. After a while, he walked his boss back to his car. They passed the pine tree, and the foreman's curiosity got the better of him. He asked the carpenter about the "tree ritual" he had seen him do earlier.

"Oh, that's my trouble tree," he replied. "I know I can't help having troubles on the job, but one thing is for sure, troubles and frustrations shouldn't be brought home at the end of the day. So, I stop by that pine tree over there and visualize hanging on it whatever troubles, frustrations and worries I have. A smile twinkled as he said, "You know, a funny thing happens when I come out in the morning to pick them up again, there aren't nearly as many as I remember hanging up the night before."

## 5.
## A Smile as Warm as the Sun

### Beth Schoentrup

It had been a long day at work. She was the only waitress on the shift, and her customers had been particularly trying. She finally sat down to rest during a lull in business. Within seconds, the door opened and in came another customer. Back to work she went.

The fellow stood six feet, four inches tall, was pencil thin and had curly white hair. "Whaddya have?" the waitress grunted.

No response. Just a steady gaze and a wide smile.

"Sir, whaddya need?" she repeated.

The customer pulled out a well-used notepad. He wrote a note, then turned the pad toward her.

"I'm deaf," was written on it, along with a question about directions. She wrote a reply. He fired off another question and another and another.

The waitress found herself smiling, introducing him to the other customers, laughing and swapping stories. The last page on his pad was a "smiley" face and the words, "Your smile is as warm as the sun."

They shook hands. He took his now-filled notepad and left the diner. Her heart was overflowing when she turned back to her customers. She really started listening to them, responding to them, loving them.

# 6.
# A Mother's Paraphrase of 1 Corinthians 13

## Mrs. Mervin Seashore

Though I speak with the language of educators and psychiatrists and have not love, I am become as blaring brass or a crashing cymbal.

And if I have the gift of planning my child's future and understanding all the mysteries of the child's mind and have ample knowledge of teenagers, and though I have all faith in my children, so that I could remove their mountains of doubts and fears and have not love, I am nothing.

And though I bestow all my goods to feed and nourish them properly, and though I give my body to backbreaking housework and have not love, it profits me not.

Love is patient with the naughty child and is kind. Love does not envy when a child wants to move to grandma's house because "she is nice."

Love is not anxious to impress a teenager with one's superior knowledge.

Love has good manners in the home—does not act selfishly or with a martyr complex, is not easily provoked by normal childish actions.

Love does not remember the wrongs of yesterday and love thinks no evil—it gives the child the benefit of the doubt.

Love does not make light of sin in the child's life (or in her own, either), but rejoices when he or she comes to a knowledge of the truth.

Love does not fail. Whether there be comfortable surroundings, they shall fail; whether there be total communication between parents and children, it will cease; whether there be good education, it shall vanish.

When we were children, we spoke and acted and understood as children, but now that we have become parents, we must act maturely.

Now abides faith, hope and love—these three are needed in the home. Faith in Jesus Christ, eternal hope for the future of the child and God's love shed in our hearts, but the greatest of these is love.

# 7.
## Grow Great by Dreams

### Anonymous

The question was once asked of a highly successful businessman, "How have you done so much in your lifetime?"

He replied, "I dream. You see, I turned my mind loose to imagine what I wanted to do. Then I went to bed and thought about my dreams. In the night, I dreamt about my dreams. And when I arose in the morning, I saw the way to make my dreams real. While other people were saying, 'You can't do that; it isn't possible,' I was well on my way to achieve what I wanted."

As Woodrow Wilson, twenty-eighth president of the United States, said: "We grow great by dreams. All big men are dreamers. They see things in the soft haze of a spring day or in the red glow of a fireplace on a long winter's evening. Some of us let these great dreams die, but others nourish and protect them—nourish them through bad days until they bring them to the sunshine and light that always comes to those who sincerely hope that their dreams will come true."

So please, don't let anyone steal your dreams or try to tell you they are impossible.

*Sing your song, dream your dream,*
*Hope your hope and pray your prayer.*

# 8.
## The Scoutmaster Saves the Day

### Walter MacPeek

For weeks the troop had been engaged in preparations for the Parents' Night Program. Everything was in order. The walls were filled with displays, the scouts with enthusiasm and the tables with good things to eat.

The toastmaster was running the program with ease. The crowd even sang with respectably restrained enthusiasm that typified Parents' Night.

Then it was Jimmie's time to give his oration. This was the moment he had looked forward to for many weeks. As he arose, he caught a glimpse of his mother's beaming smile and his father's stolid assured countenance. Jimmie started with a great burst of enthusiasm. He waxed eloquently, conscious that his listeners were paying him a high tribute by their rapt attention.

Then something happened. The world seemed to swim before his face. Jimmie slowed down—faltered—stopped. His face flushed, his hands sought each other frantically and in desperation he looked helplessly toward his scoutmaster.

And ever prepared, having heard that boyish masterpiece rehearsed again and again, the boy's leader supplied the missing words and the boy went on. But somehow it was different now. The masterpiece had been marred.

Jimmie paused again—and the scoutmaster prompted him again. For the remaining two minutes, the oration seemed more the scoutmaster's than Jimmie's.

But Jimmie finished it. But there was a heavy load in the heart of the boy who sat down, knowing he had failed in his speech. Disappointment was plainly etched on the face of Jimmie's mother, and a twitch of the father's face indicated a pained consciousness of shame.

The audience applauded perfunctorily, sorry for and pitying the boy whom they thought had failed.

The scoutmaster quickly got up and went to the microphone. His quiet eyes twinkled. Everyone listened intently, for he did not speak loudly. "What would he say?" was on everyone's mind.

The scoutmaster began, "I am more happy than any of you can possibly understand because of what just happened. You have seen a boy make a glorious victory out of what might have been a miserable failure.

"Jimmie had his chance to quit. To have quit would have been easy. But to finish the job, even in the face of two hundred people, required the highest kind of bravery and courage I know.

"You may someday hear a better oratorical effort, but I am confident that you will never see a finer demonstration of the spirit of our troop than Jimmie has just displayed—to play the game even under difficulties!"

The people thundered their applause. Jimmie's mother sat straight and proud. The pleased look of assurance was back on the face of the boy's father. The entire audience was enthusiastic and Jimmie, with a lump moving up his throat, leaned over to his friend sitting beside him and said, "Gee, if I can ever be that kind of a scoutmaster someday."

# 9.
# Youth
## (adapted)

## Samuel Ullman

Youth is not a time of life, it is a state of mind. It is not a matter of rosy cheeks, red lips and supple knees; it is a matter of the will, a quality of the imagination, a vigor of the emotions. It is the freshness of the deep springs of life.

Youth means a temperamental predominance of courage over timidity of the appetite, for adventure over the love of ease. This often exists in a person of sixty more than in a youth of twenty. Nobody grows old merely by living a number of years. We grow old by deserting our ideals.

Years may wrinkle the skin, but to give up enthusiasm wrinkles the soul. Worry, fear, self-distrust bows the heart and turns the spirit to dust.

Whether sixty or sixteen, there is in every human being's heart the lure of wonder, the unfailing childlike appetite of what's next and the joy of the game of living. In the center of your heart and my heart there is a wireless station: so long as it receives messages of beauty, hope, cheer, courage and power from men and women and from the Infinite, so long are you young.

When the aerials are down and your spirit is covered with the snows of cynicism and the ice of pessimism, then you are grown old, even at twenty, but as long as your aerials are up to catch waves of optimism, there is hope you may die young at eighty.

# 10.
# A Student's Creed

## Anonymous

Today, this new day, I am a successful student. Overnight, my mind and body have produced thousands of new cells to give me the greatest advantages possible. I am born anew, revitalized and full of energy.

I am rare and valuable; unique in all the universe. I am nature's greatest miracle in action. I have unlimited potential. I believe in my abilities, attitudes and goals. I am worthy of greatness because I am the most important person in my world.

Today I push myself to new limits. I use my skills and knowledge every day. I begin the day with a success and end it with a success. My goals are being reached every day, and I seek them eagerly.

I act positively and happily, fully accepting myself and others. I live to the fullest by experiencing life without limits. I embrace life. I approach each class, each book and each assignment with enthusiasm, happiness and joy. I thirst for knowledge. I look forward to reading and believing this creed each and every day.

I am a positive and successful student. I know each step I must take to continue to be that way. I am clear on my goals and see myself reaching them. I now realize my infinite potential; thus, my burden lightens. I smile and laugh. I have become the greatest student in the world.

# 11.
## Family Is a Garden

### Brian Cavanaugh, T.O.R.

Celebrating the feast of the Holy Family is a time to look at Joseph, Mary and Jesus as a R.E.A.L. family, an earthly family, not a pious, out-of-this-world type of family. They are a family that understands the great anxieties and sorrows of family life. The Holy Family is our model of how a family can be holy and R.E.A.L. By R.E.A.L. I mean *Respecting-Encouraging-Affirming-Loving* (attributed to Gene Wallace).

It's been said that the family is a garden and that whatever is planted in it will grow. Planting these four values in your family will bring forth a harvest of an abundant family life. I am reminded also that there exists the Law of the Fallow Field. Simply stated, this law holds that if nothing positive is planted in the garden, it will always revert to weeds. Yes, we have to continually plant each growing season exactly what it is we expect to grow; if nothing of value is planted, nothing of value will be harvested.

So here are some suggestions for your family garden:

A family, like a garden, needs…

- time, attention and cultivation.
- sunshine of laughter and affirmation.
- the rains of difficulties, tense moments of anxieties and serious discussions on important matters.
- areas of hardness to be turned over—bitterness, envy, anger, unforgiven hurts.

In this family garden, plan to plant seventeen rows…

- 5 rows of *P*s: *Perseverance, Politeness, Praise, Peacemaking* and *Prayer.*
- 4 rows of *Let us*: *Let us* be faithful in word and deed; *Let us* be unselfish with our resources; *Let us* be loyal; *Let us* love one another.

- 3 rows of *Squash: Squash* gossip; *Squash* criticism; and *Squash* indifference.
- 5 rows of *Turn ups: Turn up* on time for school plays, scout meetings and baseball games; *Turn up* for family gatherings; *Turn up* with a better attitude; *Turn up* with new ideas and the determination to carry them out; and *Turn up* with a smile.

If you plant and nurture these "value seeds" in your family garden, you will bring to a bountiful harvest a R.E.A.L. family, as well as a holy family.

## 12.
## Green Boughs and Singing Birds

### William Arthur Ward

A Chinese proverb expresses this truth: "If I keep a green bough in my heart, the singing bird will come."

Here are five "green boughs" we should strive to keep in our hearts:

The green bough of *Enthusiasm*. Enthusiasm is not only contagious, it is attractive. The singing bird of success is drawn toward the green bough of enthusiasm. Where there is enthusiasm there is excitement, and where there is positive excitement there is more joy in the job, more sparkle in the eye and more zest in living.

The green bough of *Kindness*. Kindness is the Golden Rule in action. Surely, what the world needs now is more kindness. The green boughs of kindness grow from the tree of love, and when we truly love others kindness is natural and instinctive. We should remember the little girl's prayer: "God, help the bad people be good...and please help the good people to be nice."

The green bough of *Generosity.* Our lives sing with joy when we generously share ourselves, our talents and our resources in loving service to others. Generosity is the secret of happiness; it is the golden key that unlocks the gates of joy, fulfillment and life more abundant.

The green bough of *Humor.* It has been said that if we learn to laugh at ourselves we will always be amused. The green bough of humor helps us to laugh at ourselves even when we make a faux pas, when we goof up, when we trip over our tongues or when we write something similar to this brief advertisement: "Good used typewriter for sale by secretary with wide carriage."

The green bough of *Gratitude.* Green boughs of gratitude provide the perfect home for the bluebirds of happiness. With gratitude in our hearts, there can be no room for self-pity, resentment or bitterness. Gratitude attracts more blessings—especially when we humbly and joyfully express our thanksgiving to our God and to those who have encouraged and inspired us.

# 13.
# If Jesus Came to Your House

## Anonymous

Imagine you had a dream that Jesus arrived in your town and was approaching your street. Ask yourself these pointed questions:

If Jesus came to your home to spend a day or two,
If he came unexpectedly, I wonder what you'd do.
I know you'd give your nicest room to such an honored
    guest,
And all the food you'd serve him would be the very best.

And you would keep assuring him you're glad to have him
there,
That serving him in your own home is joy beyond compare;
But when you saw him standing there, could you go to the
door,
With arms outstretched to welcome him, your heavenly visi-
tor?
Or would you have to change some things before you let him
in?
Or hide some magazines and put the Bible where they had
been?
Would family conversation be continued at its pace?
And would you find it hard each meal to say table grace?
Would you be glad to have him meet your closest friends?
Or would you hope they'd stay away until his visit ends?
Would you be glad to have him stay forever, on and on?
Or would you sigh with great relief when he at last was gone?
It might cause some embarrassment the things that you
would do,
If Jesus came to your house to spend some time with you.

## 14.
## Dear Stella

### Anonymous

Dear Stella:

I'm writing this letter slow because I know you can't
read fast. We don't live where we did when you left home to
go off to college. Your dad read in the newspaper that most
accidents happen within twenty miles from your home, so we
moved. I won't be able to send you the address because the
last family that lived here took the house numbers when they
moved so that they wouldn't have to change their address.

This place is real nice. It even has a washing machine. I'm not sure it works too well though. Last week I put a load in, pulled the chain and haven't seen them since.

The weather isn't bad here. It only rained twice last week: the first time for three days and the second for four days.

The coat you wanted me to send you, your Uncle Stanley said would be too heavy to send in the mail with the buttons on, so we cut them off and put them in the pockets.

John locked his keys in the car yesterday. We were worried because it took him two hours to get me and your father out.

Your sister had a baby this morning, but I haven't found out what it is yet so I don't know if you are an aunt or an uncle.

Uncle Ted fell in a whiskey vat last week. Some men tried to pull him out, but he fought them off and drowned. We had him cremated and he burned for three days.

Three of your friends went off a bridge in a pickup truck. Ralph was driving; he rolled down the window and swam to safety. Your other two friends were in back; they drowned because they couldn't get the tailgate down.

There isn't much more news at this time. Nothing much has happened.

Love, Mom

PS: I was going to send you some money but the envelope was already sealed.

# 15.
## The Boy's Nail Post

## Anonymous

A father wanted his son to really understand the importance of making right choices, of obeying and doing what's correct. And so if his son made a bad choice or a wrong decision, he'd give him a hammer and a nail to take out into the backyard and pound into a fence post.

Every day that the son went through the whole day making good decisions, he'd let the boy go out and remove one of those nails. Until the boy was fifteen, there were always two or three nails in the post—seems he'd be nailing new ones in as often as he'd pull others out.

The youth started to mature and make better decisions, and finally one day all the nails were removed from the post. That was when his dad took him out back and said, "I want you to notice something about the fence post."

The son looked at the post for a moment and realized that all the nails that once were driven in and then later removed had left small holes in the post. The holes were the remaining effects of the nails.

His dad said, "I want to tell you something, son, about bad choices or decisions. Even though you may be totally forgiven from your bad choices or decisions, and there are no nails visible, there are the remaining effects, the consequences, of those choices or decisions; just like the holes in that fencepost."

## 16.
## I Want to Be Possible

## Anonymous

The principal visited the first grade and asked the students, "What do you want to be when you grow up?"

A hand shot up. "I want to be possible," the boy answered.

"Possible?" the principal asked. "Of all the things you might be, why do you want that?"

The lad replied, "Because my mother and father are always saying that I'm impossible."


## 17.
## She Never Saw the Cake

## Joe Walker

Cindy glanced nervously at the clock on the kitchen wall. Five minutes before midnight. "They should be home any time now," she thought as she put the finishing touches on the chocolate cake she was frosting. It was the first time in her twelve years she had tried to make a cake from scratch and, to be honest, it wasn't exactly an aesthetic triumph. The cake was...well, lumpy. And the frosting was bitter, as if she had run out of sugar or something. Which, of course, she had.

And then there was the way the kitchen looked. Imagine a huge blender filled with all the fixings for chocolate cake—including the requisite bowls, pans and utensils. Now imagine that the blender is turned on. High speed. With the lid off. Do you get the idea?

But Cindy wasn't thinking about the mess. She had created something, a veritable phoenix of flour and sugar rising out of the kitchen clutter. She was anxious for her parents to return home from their date so she could present her anniversary gift to them. She turned off the kitchen lights and waited excitedly in the darkness. When at last she saw the flash of the car headlights, she positioned herself in the kitchen doorway. By the time she heard the key sliding into the front door, she was THIS CLOSE to exploding.

Her parents tried to slip in quietly, but Cindy would have none of that. She flipped on the lights dramatically and trumpeted: "Ta-daaa!" She gestured grandly toward the kitchen table, where a slightly off-balance two-layer chocolate cake awaited their inspection.

But her mother's eyes never made it all the way to the table. "Just look at this mess!" she moaned. "How many times have I talked to you about cleaning up after yourself?"

"But Mom, I was only…"

"I should make you clean this up right now, but I'm too tired to stay up with you to make sure you get it done right," her mother said. "So you'll do it first thing in the morning."

"Honey," Cindy's father interjected gently, "take a look at the table."

"I know—it's a mess," his wife said coldly. "The whole kitchen is a disaster. I can't stand to look at it." She stormed up the stairs and into her room, slamming the door shut behind her.

For a few moments Cindy and her father stood silently, neither one knowing what to say. At last she looked up at him, her eyes moist and red. "She never saw the cake," she said.

Unfortunately, Cindy's mother isn't the only parent who suffers from *situational timbercular glaucoma*—the occasional inability to see the forest for the trees. From time to time we all allow ourselves to be blinded to issues of long-term significance by stuff that seems awfully important right now, but isn't. Muddy shoes, lost lunch money and messy kitchens are troublesome, and they deserve their place among life's frustrations. But what's a little mud—even on a new carpet—compared to a child's self-esteem? Is a lost dollar more valuable than a youngster's emerging dignity? And while kitchen sanitation is important, is it worth the sacrifice of tender feelings and relationships?

I'm not saying that our children don't need to learn responsibility or to occasionally suffer the painful consequences of their own bad choices. Those lessons are vital and need to be carefully taught. But as parents, we must never forget that we're not just teaching lessons—we're teaching children. That means there are times when we really need to see the mess in the kitchen.

And times when we need to see only the cake.

# 18.
# A Child's Future

## Anonymous

Whether children grow up to be persons motivated by hope for success or hampered by fear of failure is often determined in their childhood. This was the conclusion reached by two doctors after surveying high school students.

It was found that young people, when stimulated by hope, tend to go ahead trying to do things, anticipating approval and reward. But when they are dominated by fear, they avoid taking action so as not to be punished for failure.

Not only children, but people of all ages and circumstances respond to encouragement and reassurance. Misgivings about their ability to make a positive contribution to life often demoralizes them. Focus more attention on their achievements than on their blunders and you will do much to bring out their hidden talent.

# 19.
## Why Build You...

### Anonymous

An old man going down a lone highway
Came at the evening cold and gray
To a chasm vast and deep and wide,
Through which was flowing a swollen tide.
The old man crossed in the twilight dim;
That swollen stream held no fears for him,
But he paused when safe on the other side
And built a bridge to span the tide.

"Old man," said a fellow pilgrim near,
"You are wasting strength with building here.
Your journey will end with the ending day;
You never again must pass this way.
You have crossed the chasm deep and wide;
Why build you the bridge at the eventide?"

The builder lifted his old gray head,
"Good friend, in the path I have come," he said,
"There follows after me today
A youth whose feet must pass this way.
This swollen stream which was naught to me
To that fair-haired youth may a pitfall be.
He, too, must cross in the twilight dim.
Good friend, I am building the bridge for him."

# 20.
# God the Earthmaker

## Edward Hays

There is a Native American creation story from the Maidu Indians of California. God the Earthmaker took some red clay, mixed it with water and carefully shaped man and woman. They were beautiful but unfinished, for they lacked hands. Earthmaker asked the other creatures what kind of hands they should have. The turtle said, "Like mine, so they can swim." And the coyote spoke up, "No, like mine, so they can run fast."

Earthmaker thought and thought and then said, "Thank you all, but I've decided to make their hands like mine so that they can make things." Since Earthmaker's hands were the pattern for human hands, women and men became the most beautiful of all creatures because they could create things with their hands.

The Maidu Indians knew what we have to remember. Our hands are godly in design and so should be busy making as God makes. They should not be hands that hold others back or hands that hold others down, "heavy" hands that prevent freedom, even the freedom to make mistakes. They should be hands busy with making peace, not clenched in anger, but waving away injury in movements of pardon. As Earthmaker's hands left fingerprints of beauty on all creation, our hands should be busy making our surroundings beautiful, clean and delightful.

And you? What are you making with your hands?

# 21.
## Jesus Focuses on the Possibilities

## Brian Cavanaugh, T.O.R.

There is a saying that some people see only the problem, while others focus on the possibility. This saying brings to mind one of my favorite verses by Reverend Charles Cummings, O.C.S.O.: "I live with a stronger hope for the possibilities that lie hidden within things, situations and persons."

This idea of *hidden possibilities* demonstrates how Jesus looks at people. He does not only see what a man or woman is; Jesus focuses also on what a man or woman can yet become. He sees not only the present reality of each person's life, he sees also the *hidden possibilities* for the future.

Jesus' decisions in choosing his apostles reflects his vision to see each person's potential. He looked at Peter and saw in him not only a Galilean fisherman, but a man who had it in him to become the rock on which Jesus would build his church. Jesus sees each of us not only as we are, but as we can still yet be. He says to us, "Give your life to me, and I will make you what you have it in you to become."

A story about seeing the hidden possibilities is told about Michelangelo working in his studio when a young boy interrupted him while he was chipping away with his mallet and chisel on a huge, shapeless block of granite. The boy asked the sculptor what he was doing. Michelangelo told him, "Can't you see it?" He then picked up the boy and stood him on the workbench. "There's an angel trapped in this rock. I'm chipping away all the pieces that are not the angel so I can set it free."

Jesus is the master craftsman who sees and sets free the *hidden possibilities* in every man or woman, boy or girl, son or daughter.

# 22.
# The School Crossing Guard

## Anonymous

"Old Bill" was hired as a school crossing guard. Every morning and every afternoon "Old Bill" manned his corner, leading the children across the street, back 'n' forth to school and home. Bill was a friendly old fellow, and every holiday the children loaded his pockets with cards and good wishes. Mrs. Franklin, whose house was on the corner where Bill worked, got into the habit on hot afternoons of bringing Bill a tall, cold glass of fresh lemonade and a few cookies.

Bill thanked her shyly and waited for the children. Then one day there was a knock at Mrs. Franklin's side door. There stood "Old Bill" with a sack of peaches in one hand and a bag with a dozen fresh-picked ears of corn in the other. He seemed embarrassed as he said, "I brought you these, Ma'am, for your kindness."

"Oh, you shouldn't have," exclaimed Mrs. Franklin. "It was nothing really, but some lemonade and cookies."

Then the crossing guard said, "Maybe it wasn't much to you, really. But, Ma'am, it was more than anyone else did for me. So, thank you."

# 23.
# The Christmas Spider

## Anonymous

In the Daily Study Bible series, William Barclay relates a lovely legend recalling when Joseph and Mary and Jesus were on their way to Egypt. As the legend goes, when evening came they were weary, and they sought refuge in a cave. It was very cold, so cold that the ground was white with hoarfrost. Now, a little spider saw the baby Jesus, and it wished so much that it could do something to keep the baby warm during the cold night. The spider decided to do the only thing it could and spun its web across the entrance of the cave to make, as it were, a curtain there.

Along came a detachment of Herod's soldiers, seeking children to kill in order to carry out Herod's bloodthirsty order. When they came to the cave entrance they were about to burst in to search it, but their captain noticed the spider's web covered with white hoarfrost stretched across the entrance to the cave. "Look, at the spider's web there," he said. "It is unbroken, so there cannot possibly be anyone in the cave, for anyone entering would certainly have torn the web."

So the soldiers passed on and left the holy family in peace, because a little spider had spun its web across the entrance to the cave.

And that, so they say, is why to this day we put tinsel on our Christmas trees, for the glittering tinsel streamers stand for the spider's web, white with the hoarfrost, stretched across the entrance of the cave in which the Holy Family stopped and found shelter on the way to Egypt.

It is a lovely story, and this much, at least, is true: no gift that Jesus receives is ever forgotten.

# 24.
## Is Your Family Holy?

### Mitch Finley

"When the Bible says *holy* it means 'separate' or 'different.' The word implies being healthy and whole in a world where much is unhealthy and fragmented. The English phrase 'hale and hearty' sums up true holiness.

"Holiness includes such concepts as humor and laughter, compassion and understanding, and the capacity to forgive and be forgiven, to love and be loved. That's holiness.

"Holy families are not free from conflict, nor do they never hurt one another. Holiness in families, rather, comes from learning to forgive and to be reconciled, and learning to face our problems and do something about them.

"In family life, *holy* means striving to surrender to God's light within us when the darkness around us seems overwhelming. It means struggling day after day to bring creative order—if only a bit of it—to the chaos in our lives. When we work at cultivating forgiveness, reconciliation and community, we embody God's holy will in the context of family life.

"A family embodies holiness by striving to be 'hale and hearty,' not by trying to be 'perfect' according to a set of otherworldly standards."

# 25.
## Gratitude Is Greater Than Practical

### Jacqueline Lowery-Corn

"Really, I don't know why I even keep trying," Julie said to her friend. They sat in the cafe of the local shopping mall just a week before Christmas. Julie sighed, "I mean, I'll spend all this time, energy and money to find my mother-in-law a Christmas gift, and she won't like it."

Her friend answered, "You haven't even bought it yet. How can you be so sure?"

"Easy. She never likes anything we give her." Julie said. "She never likes anything anybody gives her. Every holiday or birthday, it's the same thing. She mumbles a weak thank-you, if you're lucky. Then, a day or two later, you get a call. 'I was wondering,' she'll say, 'do you still have the receipt? I really need something more practical, like house slippers.'"

Julie went on, "So you give her the receipt, and she returns the gift. And if you give her practical things…she finds another reason to return them—wrong color, wrong size, wrong something. Grandma Snyder *never* accepts a gift!"

Julie's friend knew she was not exaggerating. Her mother-in-law was a wonderful woman, always baking something special to share, buying gifts for her grandchildren or offering to baby-sit or help out. But when it came to gifts or compliments, she simply could not and would not accept one graciously.

Julie finally bought a beautiful snow dome—with a full nativity scene, including the Wise Men—something her mother-in-law could enjoy for years to come.

After the holidays Julie and her friend got together again. "It was our best Christmas ever!" Julie said excitedly. "Grandma Snyder liked our gift—the snow dome! A few days after Christmas," Julie explained, "she called to tell me what a wonderful gift the snow dome was."

Several months later, at a birthday party for Julie's four-year-old daughter, Julie's friend found out what had brought about the change in Grandma Snyder. The birthday girl was having a temper tantrum because the gift of a longed-for rain-coat was not in her favorite color. So Grandma Snyder took her to the living room for a little "time out."

The friend passed by the room and saw the two of them rocking together—the child cuddled up on Grandma Snyder's lap.

"Now, Jenny, you mustn't cry because people don't give you what you thought you wanted," Grandma Snyder chided. "I used to do that—always wanting something different—until I got that snow dome from your family last Christmas. As I kept turning it over and watching the snow fall on the nativity scene, I realized that if Jesus and Mary and Joseph could accept the gifts of the shepherds and Wise Men, even though those gifts may not have seemed too practical at the time, well, so would I."

# 26.
## Sadako and the 1,000 Paper Cranes

## Anonymous

In 1945, Sadako was two years old when American planes dropped atomic bombs on Hiroshima (August 6) and Nagasaki (August 9).

By the time she was nine years old, Sadako had dreams of becoming a champion runner. To reach her goal she would practice every day. And with each passing day Sadako seemed to become stronger and faster.

Suddenly one day Sadako fell. Her teacher decided to call her parents, who rushed Sadako, against her will, to the hospital. Over the next few days, dizziness came over her more often. Sadako and her parents were soon to hear the most frightening phrase known those days in Hiroshima— atomic poisoning. Leukemia was the result of the radiation that was stored in the bodies of those who survived the "Flash," as the people of Hiroshima referred to the bomb blast. It was the most feared illness of all.

One day, Chizuko, Sadako's best friend, came to visit her at the hospital, holding her hands behind her back as she entered the room. She moved her arms around and held high in the air a piece of paper that had been carefully folded into the shape of a crane.

Sadako thanked her friend. "It isn't simply a gift," Chizuko said. "It is for good luck and health. I read a fable that the crane supposedly lives for a thousand years, and any sick person who folds a thousand paper cranes will get well." Chizuko grabbed a chair and giggled, "Let's get started!" Hands moving slowly at first and then more quickly, Chizuko began to teach Sadako how to fold the crane out of a scrap of paper.

With the help of her friend, Sadako finally folded several cranes that afternoon. Strangely, she felt better. In the days that followed, Sadako folded many more cranes. They hung from the ceiling and soon filled every nook and cranny in her hospital room. Everyone started saving paper for her cranes. At times Sadako was so weak that it was impossible for her to lift her arms. Then suddenly she would have a burst of energy and her hands quickly folded beautiful cranes again: 300-350-400.

Soon the time between completing cranes became longer for Sadako. She was determined, however, and the toll crept higher: 450-500-550-600. But Sadako got weaker every day. Now her progress was counted by fives rather than fifties: 610-615-620.

Finally, one night Sadako's strength gave out. She closed her eyes and did not open them again. Sadako had fallen short of her goal.

Chizuko and other classmates of Sadako got together and folded the remaining paper cranes, and threaded them into a wreath that was placed over Sadako's body. Not long after, Sadako's classmates, with their teacher's help, raised money for building a Children's Monument to be placed in Hiroshima's Peace Park as a reminder of what the "Flash" had done to the children.

Today, on a large pedestal of granite, stands the figure of Sadako, a golden crane perched on her outstretched hand. People from all over the world have sent hundreds and hundreds of paper crane wreaths that are draped over the granite figure. And at the base of the monument, there are these words from the children: "This is our cry, this is our prayer: Let there be peace in the world."

## 27.
## Are You Going to Help Me?

### Mark V. Hansen

In 1989 an 8.2 earthquake almost flattened Armenia, killing over thirty thousand people in less than four minutes.

In the midst of utter devastation and chaos, a father left his wife securely at home and rushed to the school where his son was supposed to be, only to discover that the building was as flat as a pancake.

After the traumatic initial shock, he remembered the promise he had made to his son. "No matter what, I'll always be there for you!" And tears began to fill his eyes. As he looked at the pile of debris that once was the school, it looked hopeless, but he kept remembering his commitment to his son.

He began to concentrate on where he walked his son to class at school each morning. Remembering his son's classroom would be in the back right corner of the building, he rushed there and started digging through the rubble.

As he was digging, other forlorn parents arrived, clutching their hearts, saying: "My son!" "My daughter!" Other well-meaning parents tried to pull him off of what was left of the school saying, "It's too late!"

"They're dead!"

"You can't help!"

"Go home!"

"Come on, face reality. There's nothing you can do!"

"You're just going to make things worse!"

To each parent he responded with one line: "Are you going to help me now?" And then he proceeded to dig for his son, stone by stone.

The fire chief showed up and tried to pull him off the school's debris saying, "Fires are breaking out, explosions are happening everywhere. You're in danger. We'll take care of it. Go home." To which this loving, caring Armenian father asked, "Are you going to help me now?"

The police came and said, "You're angry, distraught and it's over. You're endangering others. Go home. We'll handle it!" To which the father replied, "Are you going to help me now?" No one helped.

Courageously, he proceeded alone because he needed to know for himself. "Is my boy alive or is he dead?" he asked.

He dug for eight hours...twelve hours...twenty four hours...thirty six hours...then, in the thirty eighth hour, he pulled back a boulder and heard his son's voice. He screamed his son's name, "ARMAND!" He heard back, "Dad!?! It's me, Dad! I told the other kids not to worry. I told 'em that if you were alive, you'd save me, and when you saved me, they'd be saved. You promised, 'No matter what, I'll always be there for you!' You did it, Dad!"

"What's going on in there? How is it?" the father asked.

"There are fourteen of us left out of thirty three, Dad. We're scared, hungry, thirsty and thankful you're here. When the building collapsed, it made a wedge, like a triangle, and it saved us."

"Come on out, boy!"

"No, Dad! Let the other kids out first, 'cause I know you'll get me! No matter what, I know you'll be there for me."

## 28.
## What It Takes to Be a Dad

### Anonymous

Read to your children.
Keep your promises.
Go for walks together.
Let your children help with household projects.
Spend time one-on-one with each child.
Tell your children about your own childhood.
Go to the zoo, museums, ball games as a family.
Set a good example.
Use good manners.
Help your children with their homework.
Show your children lots of warmth and affection.
Set clear, consistent limits.

Consider how your decisions will affect your children.

Listen to your children.

Know your children's friends.

Take your children to work.

Open a savings account for your children's college education.

Resolve conflicts quickly.

Take your children to your place of worship.

Make a kite together.

Go fly a kite together.

Get the idea?

National Fatherhood Initiative
1-800-790-DADS

## 29.
## The Empty Chair Prayer

### Anonymous

A man's daughter asked the parish priest to come and pray with her father. When the priest arrived, he found the man lying in bed with his head propped up by two pillows; an empty chair sat next to the bed. The priest believed that the father had been informed of his visit.

"I guess you were expecting my visit?" the priest asked.

"No, who are you?" replied the father.

"I'm the new associate in your parish," said the priest. "When I saw the empty chair, I figured you knew I was going to show up."

"Oh, yeah, the chair, " said the bedridden man. "Would you mind closing the door, Father?"

Puzzled, the priest shut the door. "I've never told anyone this before, not even my daughter," said the man, "but all my life I have never known how to pray. At Sunday Mass I used to hear the pastor talk about prayer, but it always went right over my head. I abandoned any attempt at prayer," the old man continued, "until one day about four years ago my best friend said to me, 'Joe, prayer is just a simple matter of having a conversation with Jesus. Here's what I suggest,' said the friend. 'Sit down and place an empty chair in front of you; now, in faith, see Jesus sitting on that chair. It's not spooky because Jesus promised to be with us always. Then speak to him and listen in the same way you're doing with me right now.'

"So, Father, you see," said the sick man, "I tried it and I've liked it so much that I do it a couple of hours every day. I'm careful, though; if my daughter saw me talking to an empty chair, she'd either have a nervous breakdown or send me to the funny farm."

The priest was deeply moved by the man's story and encouraged the old man to continue his daily prayer ritual. The priest prayed a bit with the man, anointed him with the oil of the sick and returned to the rectory.

Two nights later the daughter called to tell the priest that her father died that afternoon. "Did he appear to die in peace?" asked the priest.

"Why, yes, Father," said the daughter. "When I left the house around two o'clock, he called me over to his bedside, told me one of his corny jokes, and kissed me on the cheek."

"When I got back from the store an hour later, I found him dead. But there was something strange, Father," she said. "In fact, beyond strange; it was kinda weird. Apparently, just before Daddy died, he must've fallen because I found him with his head resting on the chair beside the bed."

# 30.
# Judgment in All Its Seasons

## Anonymous

According to an ancient fable, there was a Persian king who wanted to discourage his four sons from making rash judgments. At his command, the eldest son made a winter journey to see a mango tree across the valley. When spring came, the next oldest was sent on the same journey. Summer followed, and the third son was sent. After the youngest made his visit to the mango tree in the autumn, the king called them together and asked each son to describe the tree.

The first son said it looked like an old stump. The second disagreed, describing it as lovely—large and green. The third son declared its blossoms were as beautiful as roses. The fourth son said that they were all wrong. To him it was a tree filled with fruit—luscious, juicy fruit, like pears.

"Well, each of you is right," the old king said. Seeing the puzzled look in their eyes, the king went on to explain. "You see, each of you saw the mango tree in a different season; thus you all correctly described what you saw. The lesson," said the king, "is to withhold your judgment until you have seen the tree in all its seasons."

The wisdom of this fable might be applied to the circumstances and situations in our lives as well, to withhold judgment until we have a better understanding of all the conditions.

# 31.
## Choose One Chair

### Luciano Pavarotti

The world-renowned opera tenor Luciano Pavarotti recalls, "When I was a boy, my father, a baker, introduced me to the wonders of song. He urged me to work very hard to develop my voice. Arrigo Pola, a professional tenor in my hometown, took me on as a student. I also enrolled in a teacher's college. As graduation was nearing, I asked my father, 'Shall I be a teacher or a singer?'

"'Luciano,' my father replied, 'if you try to sit on two chairs, you will fall between them. For life, you must choose, you can only sit in one chair.'"

Pavarotti continues, "I chose one. It took seven years of study and frustration before I made my first professional appearance. It took another seven years to reach the Metropolitan Opera. And now I think, whether it's laying bricks, writing a book—whatever we choose—we should give ourselves completely to it. Commitment—that's the key. Choose one chair."

# 32.
## God Placed a Trust in Fathers

### Starlette L. Howard

God placed a trust in fathers for strength to support their family's needs, to serve them and yet to keep enough sensitivity to support the small and fragile hopes of a little child:

- To guide in gentleness, to love and to teach with corrective discipline...not with anger but with a calm mind and an active heart.

- To know that not all the pain or scratches in life can be seen from the outside and to realize that sometimes it is the inner pains a child has that need the most comfort.
- To set an example of goodness of heart, and though a father may hold a child's hand with his own calloused fingers, he will know when to hold on firmly and when to reach out gently.
- To care enough to know that love is built in small ways in shared time in the ongoing days. Sharing love and laughter are also elements of his care.
- To be so strong that he can be leaned upon, and yet wise enough to know that God awaits to help him with each decision of the mind and will.

God placed a trust in fathers to be strong in love, persistent in forgiveness, consistent in the sharing of all he has with all those he loves and to guide his children in walking uprightly before the Lord.


# 33.
# The Catharsis from Sin Treatment

## Reverend Norman Vincent Peale

Reverend Norman Vincent Peale once related that after the morning service one Sunday a woman came up to the pastor and said, "I listened to your sermon, but I want to tell you that I itch all over."

The pastor smiled and replied, "I've had many results from my sermons, but that's the most remarkable one I've ever had."

She paid no attention to the pastor but continued, "It's a strange thing. I itch a great deal, but I itch worse when I'm in church. I sometimes feel I should not come to church because I itch so badly." She continued, "I've taken it up with my doctor...I just itch all the time, and it shows as a kind of eczema on my arm." She then bared her arm and pointed, "Take a look at that."

The pastor became interested in this woman and asked for the name of her doctor. That turned out to be even more interesting. The doctor explained that this woman had a low-grade fever most of the time. It ran about one hundred degrees.

"What's wrong with her?" the pastor asked. "She says she itches all over."

"Yes," the doctor said, "she's got eczema."

"But I didn't see any evidence of it."

"Oh," the doctor replied, "it isn't on her arms. It's on her insides. It's in the mind. She has eczema of the soul."

"I never heard of that disease, " the pastor remarked.

"And you won't find it on any list of diseases," the doctor stated, "but that's what is wrong with her—eczema of the soul."

The pastor asked how she got it and the doctor replied, "This woman has a virulent, violent, evil hatred for her sister. She feels that her sister defrauded her when they probated their father's will." The doctor continued, "She hasn't spoken to her sister for twenty years now. She is absolutely foul on the inside with her hate."

"What about the temperature? What causes that?" asked the pastor.

"It is caused by the instability of her entire system," the doctor explained. "The body is trying to throw off this hate." Then he added, "As long as she has appealed to you, why don't you give her the catharsis-from-sin treatment?"

A few days later the pastor asked the lady to stop by his office for a visit. He told her, "Your doctor tells me you are filled with sin." And he explained to her the mechanism of what was going on in her soul and how it affected her body.

She listened; she struggled against it, but finally she under-stood and accepted it.

The pastor suggested that she get down on her knees and surrender her hatred, and to do this she needed to pray lovingly about her sister. She resisted. It was very difficult for her. You cannot let go of an unhealthy thought easily because it wants to master you. But finally, she turned toward the cross and prayed, "Jesus, forgive me, a sinner, and save me by your mercy. Cleanse me. Create in me a new heart."

Gently the pastor said, "That isn't enough. Tell Jesus you *love* your sister!" And that was the hardest thing for her to say.

But the day came not too long after when the two sisters walked down the aisle of the church, arm in arm. They found forgiveness and a new love for one another.

No one of us can allow the luxury of nursing evil thoughts and actions because they will ultimately destroy you from the inside out.


# 34.
# A Mother's Daughter

## Brian Cavanaugh, T.O.R.

A friend named Donna related an experience she had at lunch the other day. She glanced around the room and noticed a woman across the dining room who looked, unbelievably, just like her mother. This woman looked about the same age and even about the same dress size as her mother.

As Donna looked at the woman a second time, she real-ized that she was looking actually at a mirrored wall of the dining room. In her own reflection she had discovered her mother as well.

It seems that in our middle years we emerge as the likenesses of our parents, even though we are not aware of the transformation, in body, mind and spirit.

## 35.
## The Pastor and the Cobbler

### Anonymous

One day the newly installed pastor walked around the streets of his new parish to acquaint himself with the people in the neighborhood. One of his first stops was at the local shoemaker's shop.

The pastor talked to the cobbler, using, at times, some lofty theological language. The cobbler replied with keen understanding and deep spiritual insight that left the pastor astonished. "You shouldn't be cobbling shoes," stated the pastor. "A man with understanding and a clear manner of expressing those thoughts should not be doing such menial, secular work."

The cobbler was quick to reply, "Pastor, you better take that back now!"

"Take what back?" asked the pastor.

"Take back," responded the cobbler, "that I'm just doing menial, secular work." Becoming annoyed, the cobbler continued, "Do you see that pair of boots on the shelf? They belong to the son of the Widow Smith, whose husband died last year. She's supported by her only child, who manages to keep a roof over their heads by working outdoors every day. I hear bad weather is in the forecast, and I felt the Lord saying to me, 'Will you cobble Widow Smith's boy some shoes so he won't catch cold and come down with some sickness?' I replied, 'Certainly, Lord, I will.'"

Looking at the pastor, the cobbler said, "Pastor, now you preach sermons under God's direction, I trust. And I will cobble that boy's boots under God's direction. Then, one day, when the final rewards are given out, the Harvest Master will say to you and to me the same approving pronouncement—*'Well done, my good and faithful servant.'*"

# 36.
# Remember the Mountain!

## Anonymous

A father and his teenage son were frequently at odds with each other over those things that fathers and sons often disagree about: homework, friends, curfews, family car and so on. It seemed that the two of them could hardly say anything to each other without getting into a shouting match. Finally, the father proposed that they go on a camping trip—just the two of them—to a mountain a few hundred miles away. Puzzled, the son agreed.

For a week, father and son together forded swift streams, climbed over huge boulders, trampled through thick brush, slept under starlit skies—and talked, talked, talked. They began to understand each other as never before. They began to see each other, not just in their usual roles of domineering father and rebellious son, but as genuine human persons, each with his own individual hopes and fears and loves. The trip up the mountain was a turning point in each of their lives.

In the years that followed, they continued to disagree on many things, but on different terms now. When a problem loomed, one or the other would say, "Remember the mountain!" An ordinary mountain became their glory mountain. What began as an ordinary camping trip was transformed into a mountaintop experience.

## 37.
## Needed: Men and Women of Character

### Anonymous

The world needs men and women...
    who cannot be bought;
    whose word is their bond;
    who put character above wealth;
    who possess opinions and a strong will;
    who are larger than their vocations;
    who do not hesitate to take risks;
    who will not lose their individuality in a crowd;
    who will be as honest in small affairs as in greater;
    who will make no compromise with wrong;
    whose ambitions are not confined to their own selfish
        desires;
    who will not say they do it "because everybody else does
        it";
    who are true to their friends through good and bad,
        in adversity as well as in prosperity;
    who do not believe that shrewdness, cunning,
        and hardheadedness are the best qualities for winning
        success;
    who are not ashamed or afraid to stand for the truth when
        it is unpopular;
    who can say "no" with emphasis, although all the rest of
        the world says "yes."

# 38.
# Listen, Son!

## W. Livingston Larned

Listen, son, I'm saying this as you lie asleep, one little hand crumpled under your cheek and the blond curls damp on your forehead. I have stolen into your room alone.

Just a few minutes ago as I sat reading my paper, a stifling wave of remorse swept over me. Guiltily, I came to your bedside.

These are the things I was thinking, son: I was cross to you. I scolded you as you were dressing for school because you gave your face a mere dab with a towel. I took you to task for not cleaning your shoes. I called out angrily when you threw some of your things on the floor.

At breakfast I found fault, too. You spilled things. You gulped down your food. You put your elbows on the table. You spread butter too thick on your bread. And as you started off to play and I made for the train, you turned and waved a hand, calling out, "Good-bye, Daddy!" I frowned, and sharply replied, "Hold your shoulders back!"

Then it began all over again in the late afternoon. As I came up the road I spied you, down on your knees, playing marbles. There were holes in your socks. I humiliated you before your friends by marching you into the house. "Socks are expensive," I told you, "and if you had to buy them you would be more careful!" Imagine that, son, from a father!

Do you remember, later, when I was reading in the library, how you came in, timidly, with a sort of hurt look in your eyes? When I glanced up over my paper, impatient at the interruption, you hesitated at the door. "What is it you want?" I snapped.

You said nothing, but ran across the room in one tempestuous plunge and threw your arms around my neck and kissed me. Your small arms tightened with an affection that God had set blooming in your heart and which even my neglect could not wither. Then you were gone, pattering up the stairs.

Well, son, it was shortly afterwards that my paper slipped from my hands and a terrible sickening fear came over me. What has habit been doing to me? The habit of faultfinding, of reprimanding—this was my reward to you for being a boy. It was not that I didn't love you; it was that I expected too much of youth. I was measuring you by the yardstick of my own years.

There is so much that is good and fine and true in your character. The little heart of yours is as big as the dawn itself over the mountain. This is shown by your spontaneous impulse to rush in and kiss me good-night. Nothing else matters tonight, son. I come to your bedside in the darkness, and kneel here ashamed!

It is a feeble atonement. I know you would not understand these things if I told them to you during your waking hours. But tomorrow I will be a real daddy! I will chum with you, and suffer when you suffer, and laugh when you laugh. I will bite my tongue when impatient words come to me. I will keep saying as if it were a ritual: "He is nothing but a boy—a little boy!"

I am afraid I have visualized you as a man. Yet as I see you now, my son, crumpled and weary in your bed, I see that you are still a child. Yesterday you were in your mother's arms, your head on her shoulder. I have asked too much, too much.

# 39.
# Heart of Gold
## (adapted)

## Florence Myles

It was Thanksgiving. No delicious smells of turkey roasting, no pies on the sideboard, no festive table setting. The mother had lost her job a few weeks ago and a daughter's tiny salary went to pay the rent. A son was still in school, and with no father in the home, things looked bleak. The mother was making a stew and had wrapped day-old bread in a paper sack and set it to warming in the oven. When the doorbell rang, the mother panicked. She was proud and didn't want anyone to know how bad things were.

When she opened the door, there stood Mr. Gold, a door-to-door salesman who kept everyone supplied with household items....Now here he stood with his arms full of grocery bags and a shy smile on his face. "Can I come begging to you today?" he asked. "Here it is Thanksgiving Day and I have no place to go and no one to share it with."

The mother was embarrassed, but invited him in and started to explain. But Mr. Gold interrupted her. "Here, I have all this food," he said. "It's only chicken, but who's to know?" And he began unpacking the groceries. There was enough for a Thanksgiving feast, from soup to nuts, plus a mincemeat and a pumpkin pie.

Mr. Gold didn't eat much, but nobody seemed to notice. When he was leaving, he thanked the family for taking such good care of a lonely old man that holiday.

# 40.
## Lesson from a Terrapin

### Anonymous

There was a boy who found a terrapin, more commonly known as a turtle. He started to examine it, but the turtle pulled in its head and closed its shell like a vice. The boy was upset, and he picked up a stick to try to pry it open.

The boy's uncle saw all this and remarked, "No, that's not the way! In fact, you may kill the turtle, but you'll not get it to open up with a stick."

The uncle took the terrapin into the house and set it near the fireplace. It wasn't but a few minutes until it began to get warm. Then the turtle pushed out its head, stretched out its legs and began to crawl. "Turtles are like that," said the uncle, "and people, too. You can't force them into anything. But if you first warm them up with some real kindness, more than likely they will do what you want them to do."


# 41.
## The Star Thrower
## (adapted)

### Loren Eisley

Early in the morning, while on vacation, Jed would go down to the beach to catch the sunrise. One day as he sat on the cool sand, he watched shell collectors aggressively engaged in a kind of greedy madness to out-collect one another. Jed watched them scrambling along the beach with sacks of gathered starfish, hermit crabs, urchins, driftwood, sea glass and such. Arguing and toppling over each other, they rushed to outdo each other to gather the finest specimens.

Jed reflected on what he had seen that morning. He thought about how many people go through life with the collectors' mentality. They are not unique to the seashore. They are in every city and in every home. They are the people who are trying to collect life and control happiness.

The next day, after spending some time gazing at the splendid sunrise, Jed noticed a solitary man walking along the water's edge, amid the frantic scurrying of the collectors. The man would stoop over, then stand up to fling an object out to sea beyond the breaking surf. Jed got up to follow him. Finally reaching the man, Jed asked him what he was doing. The man with a bronzed, weathered face softly answered, "I'm a star thrower!"

Not quite understanding what he meant, Jed got closer, expecting to see a sand dollar or perhaps a flat piece of shell—like the ones he sometimes would skip across the water. The man, with a quick yet gentle motion, scooped up another starfish and flung it far out over the waves. "It may live," the man said, "if the off-shore tide is strong enough."

Here was a human being who was not a collector, nor a spectator. He decided to become part of life and had dedicated himself to helping give back another day, another week, another year, another opportunity for living. Jed started back up the beach, back to his towel. Without realizing it, he found himself reaching down and flinging a still-living starfish out over the waves to freedom. He turned and looked back down the beach. Against the ocean's rainbow mist, the old star thrower stooped down, rising yet again to fling once more. Jed understood the man's secret now.

The star thrower's secret is sage advice for each of us to discover and live by. Life cannot be collected, nor observed from the sidelines. Life is to be celebrated by joining in, and returning or giving something back to life.

## 42.
## Let the Light Shine Through

### Anonymous

Once there was an inquisitive nine-year-old girl intently listening to the Sunday Gospel from Matthew 5:13: "You are the light of the world....your light must shine before others...." The passage really caught her attention.

The preacher talked in his sermon about the light driving out the darkness; about letting our light shine before others so that we, too, can drive out the darkness and gloom around us. The preacher then proposed this question, "And how will you be a light to the world?"

The young girl's imagination clicked into gear as she thought about being a light. Her thoughts rambled until she looked at the brightly colored patterns of light shining across the pews. She leaned closer to her father and whispered, "Daddy, I want to be like a stained-glass window and let the light shine through me spreading pretty colors."

Jesus said, "In the same way, your light must shine before others so that they may see goodness in your acts and give praise to your heavenly father" (Mt 5:16).

## 43.
## Does She Have to Be So Tough?

### Brian Cavanaugh, T.O.R.

Shortly after midterm exams, a student stopped me as I was walking across campus. I asked her how her tests had gone and she said they were not too tough, except for one professor's. "Her tests are impossible to pass," she said. "I have to study so much harder for her tests just to keep up my grades."

"But," I asked, "do you learn more from all that studying for her tests, or from the teachers that are not so difficult?"

"Well, yes, I do seem to understand her course better," she explained. "But does she have to be so tough?"

So I asked her if she had ever sharpened a knife.

"Yes," she said, "my daddy taught my how to sharpen a knife when we went on a family camping trip."

"Did you use a stone or a towel?" I asked.

"What?" she questioned. "You can't sharpen a knife on a towel!"

"Exactly!" I answered. "You can't sharpen a knife on a towel. A knife can only be sharpened on a hard surface so that it will be sharp enough to fulfill its purpose and cut what needs cutting." I continued, "Students, and children, too, cannot be sharpened on soft surfaces. They are sharpened on the hard surfaces of teachers and parents, so that they will be sharp enough to 'cut it' in life and fulfill their life purpose."

# 44.
# King Solomon's Ring

## Anonymous

An old Jewish legend tells that King Solomon once asked a jeweler to design a ring and inscribe words on the ring band that would be true and appropriate at all times and in all situations.

A month later, the jeweler brought the king a ring inscribed with the words, "This too shall pass."

On bad days the king would read the inscription and be reassured, and when he was having an especially good day, the king would read it and be sobered back to reality.

# 45.
## Search for Answers to Great Questions

### Anonymous

The late anthropologist Margaret Mead relates the experience in one of her widely read books of a teenage boy who expressed his own perception of the "struggle to find love." This, in part, is what he said:

"There is mass confusion in the minds of my generation in trying to find a solution for ourselves and the world around us. We see the world as a huge rumble as it swiftly goes by with wars, poverty, prejudice and the lack of understanding among people and nations. Then we stop and think—there must be a better way, and we have to find it. If we are to be a generation of repetition, the situation will be worse. But how shall we change?

"I have yet to discover what we need. I admit we should follow some basic rules, but first we should look at who is making the rules. Sometimes I walk down a deserted beach listening to the waves and birds, and I hear them forever calling and forever crying. Sometimes we, too, feel that way. But everyone goes on with his or her own little routines of life, afraid to stop and listen. The answer is out there somewhere. We need to search for it!"

# 46.
## Why Are Things the Way They Are?

### Anonymous

One day, Mr. Reynolds, a high school junior English teacher, handed each student a list of thoughts or statements written by other students, then gave the class a creative writing assignment based on one of those thoughts. One girl, at the age of seventeen, was beginning to wonder about many things, so she chose the statement, "I wonder why things are the way they are."

That night, she wrote down in the form of a story all the questions that puzzled her about life. She realized that many of them were hard to answer, and perhaps others could not be answered at all. When she turned in her paper, she was afraid that she might fail the assignment because she had not answered the question, "I wonder why things are the way they are?" She had no answers. She had only written questions.

The next day Mr. Reynolds called her to the front of the class and asked her to read her story for the other students. He handed her the paper and sat down in the back of the room. The class became quiet as she began to read her story:

"Mommie, Daddy…Why?
Mommie, why are the roses red?
Mommie, why is the grass green and the sky blue?
Why does a spider have a web and not a house?
Daddy, why can't I play in your toolbox?
Teacher, why do I have to read?
Mother, why can't I wear lipstick to the dance?
Daddy, why can't I stay out until 12 o'clock? The other kids are.
Mother, why do you hate me?
Daddy, why don't the boys like me?
Why do I have to be so skinny?
Why do I have braces and wear glasses?
Why do I have to be sixteen?
Mom, why do I have to graduate?
Dad, why do I have to grow up?
Mom, Dad, why do I have to leave?
Mom, why don't you write more often?
Dad, why do I miss my old friends?
Dad, why do you love me so much?
Dad, why do you spoil me? Your little girl is growing up.
Mom, why don't you visit?

Mom, why is it hard to make new friends?
Dad, why do I miss being at home?
Dad, why does my heart skip a beat when he looks in my eyes?
Mom, why do my legs tremble when I hear his voice?
Mother, why is being 'in love' the greatest feeling in the world?
Daddy, why don't you like to be called 'Gramps'?
Mother, why do my baby's tiny fingers cling so tightly to mine?
Mother, why do they have to grow up?
Daddy, why do they have to leave?
Why do I have to be called 'Grannie'?
Mommie, Daddy, why did you have to leave me? I need you.
Why did my youth slip past me?
Why does my face show every smile that I have ever given to a
        friend or a stranger?
Why does my hair glisten a shiny silver?
Why do my hands quiver when I bend to pick a flower?
Why, God, are the roses red?"

At the conclusion of the story, her eyes locked with Mr. Reynolds's eyes, and she saw a tear slowly sliding down his cheek. It was then that she realized that life is not always based on the answers we receive, but also on the questions that we ask.


# 47.
## It Takes Courage to Care
(adapted)

## Arthur Gordon

It was a crowded day at the Jersey shore; the weather was hot and the beach overflowed with bathers. A woman was splashing in the surf when she accidentally stepped off the sandbar and dropped into a swift undertow that dragged her under the water. Frantically, she struggled to escape the strong current, yelling for help. At least twenty adults watched from the shoreline, apparently paralyzed, until a young man sprinted into the surf, swam out to her and helped her back to the beach.

A witness to the event described the episode to the beach patrol. He spoke of his admiration for the young man who responded so quickly, and of his contempt for all those people who stood by and failed to act. "The woman had been in a dangerous situation and those people didn't even seem to care," he grumbled.

The officer looked at the man and said, "The world often seems divided between those who care and those who don't care enough. But don't judge too harshly. It takes courage to care greatly."

# 48.
# Old Rattle Bones

## Anonymous

Many years ago there was a man, crippled and poor, who was cruelly nicknamed "Old Rattle Bones" by a group of boys in his neighborhood. The leader of the group, Freddie, was worried one day when he saw the crippled man heading right toward his home. Because his friends were with him, the boy attempted to hide his anxiety by taunting. "Go on, Old Rattle Bones," he shouted, "see if I care if you talk to my mother."

The man looked at Freddie sadly as he passed the group of boys and said, "You would not be calling me such names if you knew what caused my crippled condition." He continued along the street arriving at Freddie's home, whereupon he was warmly welcomed by Freddie's mother. She called for her son to come in also.

While the mother brought out a pot of tea, the man turned toward the boy and told him a story. "Years ago, on the first day of spring, a young mother took a baby outdoors for a carriage ride along the river. Stooping to pick a flower, she briefly let go of the handle; suddenly the carriage lurched forward, careening down the hill. Before she could catch up with the carriage, it had plunged into the river. I was sitting on a nearby bench and heard her scream. I ran after the buggy and jumped into the river. After a difficult struggle I managed to get the baby safely back to shore. I left before anyone could ask my name.

"But, you see, the river water was still very cold, and it aggravated my rheumatism. Now, ten years later, I can scarcely hobble along. For you see, Freddie, that baby was you."

Freddie hung his head in shame and began to cry. "Thank you for saving me," he wept. "Can you ever forgive me for calling you 'Old Rattle Bones'? I didn't know who you were!"

### 49.
### Press On!

## Lloyd John Ogilvie

An Olympic runner was asked the secret of his success. His answer has profound implications for the Christian life.

This is what the runner said: "The only way to win a race is to forget all previous victories, which would give you false pride, and all former failures, which would give you false fears. Each race is a new beginning. Pressing on to the finish tape is all that's important."

Forget past achievements and failures. Press on to the goal. Press on!

# 50.
# Ask the Question
## (adapted)

## Joan W. Laflamme

Martin Luther King, Jr. provided a reliable way to judge both the major and the minor issues that are part of our day-to-day living. Speaking in 1967, Dr. King said, "Cowardice asks the question, 'Is it safe?' Expediency asks the question, 'Is it politic?' Vanity asks the question, 'Is it popular?' But conscience asks the question, 'Is it right?'"

We might ask one further question, "Is it loving?" It doesn't sound difficult, but if we succeed in doing the right and loving thing today, tomorrow and each day thereafter, we will be following the "Golden Rule" principle by treating others how we would want to be treated, and treating them as such first.

# 51.
# Grains of Caring

## Anonymous

Two brothers worked together on the family farm. One was married and had a large family. The other was single. At the day's end, the brothers shared everything equally, produce and profit.

Then one day the single brother said to himself, "It's not right that we should share equally the produce and the profit. I'm alone and my needs are simple." So each night he took a sack of grain from his bin and crept across the field between their houses, dumping it into his brother's bin.

Meanwhile, the married brother said to himself, "It's not right that we should share the produce and the profit equally. After all, I'm married and I have my wife to look after me and my children for years to come. My brother has no one, and no one to take care of his future." So each night he too took a sack of grain and dumped it into his single brother's bin.

Both men were puzzled for years because their supply of grain never dwindled. Then one dark night, the two brothers bumped into each other. Slowly it dawned on them what was happening. They dropped their sacks and embraced one another.

## 52.
## A Prayer for His Son

### General Douglas MacArthur

Build me a son, O Lord,
   who will be strong enough to know when he is weak,
   brave enough to face himself when he is afraid....

Build me a son,
   whose wishes will not take the place of deeds...
   Lead him, I pray, not in the path of ease and comfort,
   but under the stress and spur of difficulties and challenges.

Let him learn to stand in the storm;
   let him learn compassion for those who fall.

Build me a son,
   whose heart is clear, whose goals will be high;
   a son who will master himself before he seeks to master
     others;
   who will reach into the future, yet never forget the past.

And after all these things are his, add, I pray,
  enough of a sense of humor
  so that he may always be serious
  yet never take himself too seriously....

Then, I, his father will dare to whisper,
  "I have not lived in vain."

# 53.
# Put God in the Center

## Mark Link, S.J.

In his book *I Believe,* Grant Teaff, former head football coach at Baylor University, tells a remarkable story. It is about a young man who was once the world's greatest pole-vaulter. His name is Brian Sternberg.

In 1963 Brian was a sophomore at the University of Washington. He was not only the world's best pole-vaulter, but also America's trampoline champion. Teaff writes, "Word around track circles, though, was that Sternberg was the most self-centered young athlete to come along in a long time."

Teaff tells how he watched Brian perform the day he broke the world's record. "The thing that caught my eye," Teaff says, "was his poise and confidence and the fact that he never smiled."

The next day, Teaff picked up the paper and was stunned. The headline read, "Brian Sternberg Injured." Brian had been working out alone in the gym. He did a triple somersault and came down on the trampoline wrong. His neck hit the edge, snapping it and leaving him totally paralyzed, able to move only his eyes and his mouth. Brian was left a helpless, hopeless cripple and a very bitter young man.

Five years later, Coach Teaff saw Sternberg again at a convention of coaches and athletes in Colorado. The auditorium was totally dark. Suddenly a projector lit up the screen, and there was Brian Sternberg racing down the runway executing that record-breaking pole vault. Every coach and athlete oohed and aahed.

Then the auditorium went totally dark again, except for a single spotlight shining on a single chair on the empty stage. Out of the shadows emerged a huge football player carrying in his arms what looked like a big rag doll. Its long arms and legs hung limp at its sides and flopped this way and that. The rag doll was six-foot, three-inch Brian Sternberg, who now weighed eighty-seven pounds.

Sternberg was placed in the chair and propped up with pillows to keep him from falling over. Then in a raspy voice Brian began to talk. He said, "My friends…Oh, I pray to God that what happened to me will never happen to one of you. I pray that you will never know the humiliation, the shame of not being able to perform one human act.

"Oh, I pray to God you will never know the pain that I live with daily. It is my hope and my prayers that what has happened to me will never happen to one of you. Unless, my friends, that is what it takes for you to put God in the center of your life."

The impact of Brian Sternberg's words was electrifying. No one there will ever forget him.


# 54.
# The Wallenda Factor
## (adapted)

## C. W. Bass

Karl Wallenda lived on top of the world—literally. The high-wire aerialist thrilled thousands with his daring stunts on the tightrope before that fateful day in 1978 when his show ended. Wallenda plunged to his death before an audience in San Juan, Puerto Rico.

What happened? His widow explained that Karl never had been one to know fear. Self-confidence marked his style, until he started worrying. Little details of safety preoccupied his mind. He checked and double-checked the tightrope to make certain that everything was secure. He even examined how the guide bolts were secured, which he had never done before.

This was a different Wallenda. For the first time, instead of focusing on walking the wire, he concentrated on *not falling*. From then on Wallenda became an accident just waiting to happen. It was inevitable that he fall, or so his widow felt.

This type of fear is now known as the Wallenda factor. Beware of being so afraid of failure that you dwell on the negatives. If so, you will succeed only in the ultimate negative, which is nothing.

Life is a risk we must take. Be careful in a prudent sort of way, but don't be paralyzed by a fear of failure.

# 55.
## A Tombstone for Mediocrity

### C. C. Mitchell

Miss Jones, an elderly spinster, lived in a small midwestern community. She had the notoriety of being the oldest resident in the town. On the day she died, the editor of the local newspaper wanted to print a brief epitaph commemorating Miss Jones's legacy. However, the more he thought about it, the more he became aware that while Miss Jones had never done anything terribly wrong (after all, she had never spent a night in jail, nor had ever been drunk), yet she had never accomplished anything of note.

While musing over this, the editor went to a local diner for his morning coffee and met the owner of the granite memorial company. He poured out his dilemma. The tombstone proprietor stated that he was having a similar problem. He wanted to put something on Miss Jones's tombstone besides, "Miss Nancy Jones, born such and such date and died such and such date," but he could not dig up anything of significance that she had ever done.

The editor finished his coffee and headed back to his office. He decided that he would assign the task of writing up a short piece suitable for both the paper and the tombstone to the first reporter he met at the paper. Upon returning, only the sports editor was in the newsroom, so he got the assignment. It is told that if you pass through that little town you will find the following epitaph carved on Miss Jones's tombstone:

*Here lies the bones of Nancy Jones,*
*For her life held no terrors.*
*She lived an old maid. She died an old maid.*
*No hits, no runs, no errors*

# 56.
# Final Fixing of the Foolish Fugitive

## Reverend W. O. Taylor

Feeling foot-free and frisky, this feather-brained fellow finagled his fond father into forking over his fortune. Forthwith, he fled for foreign fields and frittered his farthings feasting fabulously with fair-weather friends. Finally, facing famine and fleeced by his fellows in folly, he found himself a feed flinger in a filthy farmlot. He fain would have filled his frame with foraged food from fodder fragments.

"Fooey! My father's flunkies fare far fancier," the frazzled fugitive fumed feverishly, frankly facing fact.

Frustrated from failure and filled with forebodings, he fled for his family.

Falling at his father's feet, he floundered forlornly. "Father, I have flunked and fruitlessly forfeited further family favors...."

But, the faithful father, forestalling further flinching, frantically flagged his flunkies to fetch forth the finest fatling and fix a feast.

But the fugitive's fault-finding frater, faithfully farming his father's fields for free, frowned at this fickle forgiveness of former falderal. His fury flashed, but fussing was futile.

His foresighted father figured, "Such filial fidelity is fine, but what forbids fervent festivities? The fugitive is found! Unfurl the flags! With the fanfare flaring, let fun, frolic and frivolity flow freely, former failures forgotten and folly forsaken. Forgiveness forms a firm foundation for future fortitude."

# 57.
# Wake Up!

## Anonymous

There's a story about a father who knocks on his son's bedroom door. "Teddy," he calls out, "wake up!"

Teddy answers, "I don't want to get up, Papa."

The father shouts, "Get up. It's Saturday and you have to go to practice today."

Teddy shouts back, "I don't want to go to practice."

"And why not?" asks the father.

"Well, there're three reasons," says Teddy. "First, practice is so dull; second, the kids tease me; third, I hate practice, especially on Saturday."

The father leans against the door and says, "Well, I'm going to give you three reasons why you *must* go to practice. First, because it is your duty as a member of the team; second, because you are forty-five years old; and third, because you are the coach."

## 58.
## Paganini's Violin

### Anonymous

The great violinist, Nicolo Paganini, willed his exquisite violin to Genoa—the city of his birth—but only on the condition that the instrument never be played again. It was an unfortunate condition, for it is a characteristic of wood that as long as it is used and handled, it shows little decline in quality. However, as soon as it is set aside in storage, it begins to decay.

The fabulous, mellow-toned violin became worm-eaten stored in its gorgeous case, valueless now except as a relic. The deteriorating instrument is a reminder that gifts and talents are tools meant to be used, not treasures to be stored up. Likewise, a life withdrawn from love and service to others loses its meaning.

## 59.
## The Most Frequent Question

### Anonymous

Some time ago Ann Landers was asked by a reporter, "What is the question that you are asked most frequently by your readers?"

Miss Landers answered that it was a very simple question: "What's the matter with me? Why am I so lonely?"

The interviewer then asked her what her advice was for that problem. Her answer was equally as simple: "Get involved! Do something good for other people."

People who need your help are all around you. Everywhere you look, you will see them. One finds what one looks for in life. What is it you see?

## 60.
## "Second Coming" Compliant—
## A Readiness Survey
### (adapted)

### Father Peter Daly

There was a pastor who wrote about receiving a survey in the mail from the local electric company reflecting the widespread concern about the Y2K computer problems.

Among the questions on the survey, it was the last question that stumped him: "Will your essential functions be affected?"

The pastor, after some consideration, wondered just what the essential functions of the parish were. He reflected that the church is primarily a community of charity and prayer; therefore, the parish could continue its essential functions quite well. He wrote, "We should be able to celebrate the sacraments, do works of charity, study the scriptures and teach the faith, even if the computers shut down."

With further reflection the pastor mused, "We might not be able to fill in all those forms that come to us from the diocese and the government, which would be God's form of justice. We might not be able to schedule so many events, which would give us all a needed Sabbath rest."

That power company survey made the pastor then wonder about the "day of judgment" readiness of the parish community. "What if we sent out a similar survey," he contemplated, "to determine if the people in the parish are 'second coming' compliant? What essential functions would we want them to consider?"

So the pastor started to write down some points to ponder:

- Have you fed the hungry lately?
- Have you given drink to the thirsty?
- Are strangers welcomed in your community?
- What provisions have you made for clothing the naked and sheltering the homeless?
- Are your programs for visiting the sick and the imprisoned working well?
- Do you worship God in spirit and truth?
- Have you been building up one another with words of encouragement?
- Have you been reconciling enemies, making peace and comforting those who mourn?
- What have you done to reduce the violence in your community? What about reducing the violent rages within your own heart?
- In what ways have you hungered and thirsted for justice and not sought vengeance?
- Have you preached the Good News lately—by your words or your deeds?
- Have you told people of God's abundant love?
- Are your treasures stored up in heaven or in a safety deposit box?

The pastor noted, "Most of us would have a harder time filling out the second survey than the first." He continued, "I'd also be willing to bet that it would be a lot more important to get compliant with the second readiness survey."

The pastor concluded, "One way or another, we will muddle through computer glitches. But if we don't get compliant with the concerns of the Lord's survey of readiness, we might not get through the 'day of judgment' unscathed. Now that's a survey to take seriously."

# 61.
## Worry Is Like a Fog

### Anonymous

According to the National Bureau of Standards, a dense fog covering seven city blocks to a depth of a hundred feet is composed of something less than one glass of water. This can be compared to the depth of the things we worry about in life. If we could see into the future, if we could see problems in their true light, they would not blind us to the world—to living itself—but instead could be viewed in their true size and perspective. Moreover, if all the things we worry about were reduced to their true size, we could probably put them all into a single drinking glass, too.

# 62.
## Reflect a Little Sunshine

### Anonymous

In a tenement district in New York City, a boy in ragged clothes was seen with a small mirror in his hand. Holding it high in the air, he waved it back and forth, watching the narrow window many floors above him.

"What are you doing?" a man suddenly demanded as he roughly shook the youngster by the shoulder. "Like most street urchins, you're probably up to some no good mischief, aren't you?"

The boy looked up into the man's stern face and said, "See that window up there, mister? Well, I have a little brother whose room's on that floor. He's paralyzed and the only sunlight he ever sees is what I can shine up to him with my mirror!"

# 63.
# The Once Mighty Oak

## Anonymous

There was a massive tree—sort of a treasured landmark—where students had met for decades. No one could even imagine the college campus without the mighty oak that spread its giant limbs for all to enjoy. It seemed to be a perpetual part of the landscape...*until*. Then one day, with an enormous nerve-jolting C-R-A-C-K, the mighty giant crashed to the ground. Once down, all who grieved its passing could see what no one had bothered to notice over the years. A downward spiral of internal erosion, month by month, season after season, had been taking place. Just because it was silent and slow didn't mean it was not dying. The seemingly eternal mighty oak tree was hollow from years of decay. All that was seen by passers by was simply a shell of an oak tree.

What was true of the mighty oak tree can also be said for people. Ever so slightly, invisible moral and ethical decay can invade, beginning the stages of a terminal disease.

# 64.
# A Brother's Sacrifice

## Anonymous

Back in the fifteenth century, in a tiny village in Germany, lived a family with eighteen children. Despite a seemingly hopeless situation, two brothers shared a dream to pursue their talent for art. But they knew that the family's financial condition was too tight to pay for their studies.

The two boys came up with their own solution. They would toss a coin. The loser would go into the nearby mines and support his brother attending the art academy. Then that brother, at the end of his studies, would support the other brother at the academy, either with sales of his artwork or, if necessary, also by laboring in the mines.

So one brother went to the art academy while the other went into the dangerous mines. After four years the young artist returned to his village and family. There was a triumphant homecoming dinner. The artist rose from the table to drink a toast to his beloved brother for his years of sacrifice. His closing words were, "And now, Albert, it is your turn. Now you can go to the academy to pursue your dream, and I will support you."

Albert sat there, tears streaming down his face, shaking his lowered head while he sobbed and repeated over and over, "No...no...no!"

Finally, Albert rose and wiped the tears from his eyes. He looked down the long table, and holding his hands out in front of him, he said softly, "No, brother, it is too late for me to go. Look...look at what four years in the mines have done to my hands! The bones in every finger have been crushed at least once, and I've been suffering from arthritis so badly that I cannot hold even a wine glass to return your toast, much less make delicate lines on canvas with a pen or brush. No, brother, for me it is too late."

Then one day, to pay homage to Albert for all that he had sacrificed, Albrecht Dürer painstakingly drew his brother's tortured hands with palms together and crooked fingers pointed skyward. He called his powerful drawing simply *Hands,* but the entire world almost immediately opened their hearts to his masterpiece and renamed his tribute of love *The Praying Hands.*

# 65.
## Candles in the Window

### Anonymous

The custom of placing lighted candles in the windows at Christmas was brought to America by Irish immigrants. The historical background of this custom is interesting. When religion was suppressed throughout Ireland during the English persecution, the people had no churches in which to worship and celebrate the Mass. Priests hid in forests and caves, secretly visiting farms and homes to say Mass there during the night. It was the dearest wish of every Irish family that at least once in their lifetime a priest would arrive at Christmas to celebrate the Mass during the Holy Night. For this grace they hoped and prayed all through the night.

When Christmas arrived, they left all the doors unlocked and placed burning candles in the windows so that any priest who happened to be in the vicinity would be welcomed and guided to their home through the dark night. Silently the priest would enter through the unlatched door, wherein he would be received by the devout with fervent prayers of gratitude and flowing tears of happiness that their home was to become a church for Christmas.

To justify this practice in the eyes of the English soldiers, the Irish used to explain: "We burn the candles and keep the doors unlatched so that Mary and Joseph, looking for a place to stay, will find their way to our home and be welcomed with open doors and open hearts." The English authorities, finding this Irish "superstition" harmless, did not bother to suppress it. Candles in the windows have always remained a cherished custom of the Irish, although many of them have long since forgotten the earlier significance.

The custom was brought to America in the early nineteenth century and spread throughout the land, so much so that electric candles and lights of all kinds are used in homes and public squares during the Christmas season.

Light a candle in your window this Christmas season as a beacon to all that your home is a place of welcome with open doors and open hearts.


# 66.
# Looking for Something to Find

## Anonymous

During the Christmas shopping rush a mother and her four-year-old daughter were among the Christmas shoppers walking along festive Fifth Avenue in New York City. The little girl kept looking down at the sidewalk.

"Why don't you look at the store windows, all decorated and so pretty?" the mother asked as she watched her daughter staring down as they walked along the avenue.

"I'm looking for something," answered the daughter.

"What, in heaven's name, are you looking for down there?" the mother asked.

"Mother," replied the girl, "I'm looking for something to find."

Are not we all a bit like the daughter? Too often, we walk through life with our eyes fixed on the ground, looking for something to find and unaware of what is already around us.

# 67.
## People of the Beatitudes

### Anonymous

One night Jesus showed up at a meeting in the church hall. He invited the crowd to pull up chairs and gather around. When everyone was settled and comfortable, Jesus himself pulled up a chair and began to teach them:

"Blessed are they who value the love of family and friends over everything else—the brother or sister who is always there for the family, the devoted volunteer—for theirs is the kingdom of heaven.

"Blessed are they who grieve for the lost and struggle to cope and continue—the single parent trying to raise a family alone, the mother or father who keep an open heart and outreached hand to the wayward son or daughter—for they shall be comforted.

"Blessed are they who find their joy in the happiness of others—the devoted parent, the dedicated teacher—for they shall inherit the earth.

"Blessed are they who manage to see beyond their own interests and needs to the greater common good and their responsibility to others—for they shall be satisfied.

"Blessed are they who treat classmates, coworkers and employees with respect and dignity, who remember that they have been forgiven by a compassionate God and readily extend that forgiveness and compassion to others—for they shall receive mercy.

"Blessed are they who dedicate their lives to seeking God's justice and forgiveness in all things and who put themselves at the service of others to help them discover the joy of God's presence in their lives—for they shall see God.

"Blessed are the peacemakers, those who possess that rare gift for bringing people together when anger and selfishness threaten to drive them apart, who readily take the first step in forgiving and being reconciled with others, who bring healing to those who have been hurt, forgotten or marginalized—for they are the sons and daughters of God.

"Blessed are they who are persecuted and ridiculed for what is right and just, parents, teachers and dedicated individuals who stand in opposition to false perceptions, destructive stereotypes and an ever more alienated and cynical society, who speak for the needs of children and for justice for the poor, compassion for the fallen and lost, and loving support for the abused—for the reign of God is theirs.

"Be glad and rejoice," Jesus told the group that were gathered in the church hall that night, "for *your* reward in heaven is great."


## 68.
## Throwing Off the Curve

### Anonymous

There was a series of "Doonesbury" comic strips telling the story of Kim, a high school student of Asian ancestry whose hard work in school won her a coveted National Merit Scholarship.

In one panel, Kim is called into the office of the principal who tells her, "Kim, I just wanted to tell you how proud all of us are about your nomination as a Merit Scholar! It's very good news for your family and for the school. Your accomplishment demonstrates that the failure of so many kids to learn here is not just the school's fault. It reaffirms the importance of discipline and personal motivation."

"Yes, sir," Kim replied, "but I'm not so sure everyone in the community sees it quite that way."

And, sure enough, in the next panels, a group of parents are at the front door of Kim's home, confronting her father.

"She's throwing off the curve for the entire school," they complain. "How does she do so well anyway? Couldn't you get her to watch more TV like the other children?"

Kim's American father calmly explains that they've tried to instill in their daughter her culture's values of discipline, hard work and respect for others. The other parents are taken aback for a moment. A mother protests, "But doesn't that give her an unfair advantage?" Another father blusters, "Yeah, this is America!"

## 69.
## We Are Parts of the Puzzle

### Anonymous

A religion teacher brought a large poster to class one day. The picture was covered with newspaper. She took scissors and cut the covered poster into fifteen pieces. She then gave each student a piece a of the puzzle. "Take your piece home," the teacher said, "but don't peek at it. Remember to bring your piece to the next class."

The following week in religion class the teacher had the students gather around a table to put the pieces back together. Excitedly they fit them together to see what the mystery poster looked like. When all the students had placed their pieces on the table, they discovered something terrible. The poster had two gaping holes, two parts were missing. Two students forgot their pieces of the poster puzzle.

The teacher made this a teaching moment by explaining to the class, "Jesus told us to be his disciples. And when one of us fails to do his part, Jesus' witness in the world loses some of its luster, just like this poster with two of its parts missing."

In baptism each disciple of Jesus was given a piece of the puzzle. What have you done with your piece? Do you know where it is? Pray that each of us does not lose our piece to Jesus' puzzle of discipleship and leave a big gaping hole in the world.

## 70.
## Face-to-Face, Heart-to-Heart
## (adapted)

### Mary Best

A few years ago at a Marriage Encounter weekend, a couple asked the group for prayers for their marriage, which was undergoing some serious trials. Before praying, the weekend leader suggested that the couple find a quiet place apart where they, before the day was over, could, face-to-face, tell one another, honestly and gently, just what it was that the other was doing that was causing so much pain and hurt.

When the leader paused and before he could say anything further, his wife quietly interjected, "Believe me, he is not just talking marriage counseling theory. Many years ago, we were at a similar point in our marriage. We did just this same thing with copious tears and a great deal of pain. But, let me tell you, it works!"

## 71.
## Formula for a Successful Marriage

### Anonymous

A reporter, interviewing a couple who were nearing their fiftieth wedding anniversary, asked them the secret for their long and successful marriage. The husband said that he learned the secret from his father-in-law.

A few weeks before the day of the wedding, the young man asked his future father-in-law what he could do to make his wife-to-be happy. He received his answer in a small package given to him by his father-in-law the morning of the wedding. "This," said the father-in-law, "is all you need to know to make your marriage work."

Opening the package, the husband-to-be found a gold pocket watch. Inscribed across the cover of the watch where he would be sure to see it several times a day was the message: "Say something nice to Sarah."

It seems simple enough to do, but from your own family life you are probably aware that compliments and praise are not always part of the daily routine. However, they very easily could be if we acted upon our intuitions more often. It's just that family is generally, and too often, taken for granted. Consequently, little things are overlooked. Yet it's those little things that make strong and lasting bonds.

A daily compliment is a small enough thing. Let the encouragement of others spring to your lips freely and easily. St. Augustine gave some sage advice when he said, "You aspire to great things? Begin with little ones."

## 72.
## Irish Wedding Blessing

### Anonymous

May the road rise to meet you.
May the wind be always at your back.
May the sun shine warm upon your face,
The rains fall soft upon your fields.
May the light of friendship guide your paths together.
May the laughter of children grace the halls of your home.

May the joy of living for one another trip a smile from your
    lips,
A twinkle from your eye.
And when eternity beckons, at the end of a life heaped high
    with love,
May the good Lord embrace you with the arms that have
    nurtured you the whole length of your joy-filled days.
May the gracious God hold you both in the palm of his
    hands.
And, today, may the Spirit of Love find a dwelling place in
    your hearts.
Amen.

## 73.
## 17 Rules for a Happy Marriage

### Roy Burgess

1. The very nearest approach to domestic happiness on each side is the cultivation on both sides of absolute unselfishness.
2. Never both be angry at once.
3. Never speak loudly to one another unless the house is on fire.
4. Let each one strive to yield most often to the wishes of the other.
5. Let self-denial be the daily aim and practice of each partner.
6. Never find fault unless it is perfectly certain that fault has been committed, and always speak lovingly.
7. Never taunt with past mistakes.
8. Neglect the whole world rather than one another.
9. Never allow a request to be repeated.

10. Never part for a day without loving words to think of during the absence.
11. Never make a remark at the expense of each other.
12. Never let the sun go down on any anger or grievance.
13. Never meet without a loving welcome.
14. Never forget the happy hours of early love.
15. Never sigh over what might have been, but make the best of what is.
16. Never forget that marriage is ordained of God, and that His blessings alone can make it what it should be.
17. Never be content till you know both are walking in the same narrow path.

# 74.
# Only a Mother's Love

## Anonymous

The harried young mother was beside herself when the telephone rang, and she heard with relief the kindly voice on the line, "Hi, sweetheart. How are you?"

"Oh, Mother," she said, breaking into tears, "it's been an awful day. The baby won't eat, the dishwasher broke down. I tripped up the stairs and sprained my ankle. I haven't had a chance to go shopping and the house is a mess. And, to top it off, we're having company over for dinner tonight!"

"There, there, darling, everything will be all right," the soothing voice on the line said. "Now sit down, relax and close your eyes. I'll be over in a half hour. I'll pick up a few things on the way over and cook dinner for you. I'll take care of the house and feed the baby. Also, I'll call a repairman I know who will be at your house to fix the washer this afternoon. Now stop crying. I'll take care of everything. In fact,

I'll even call George at the office and tell him to come home early."

"George?" the distraught housewife exclaimed. "Who's George?"

"Why, George…you know, George, your husband!"

"But my husband's name is Frank."

A brief pause ensued, then the voice hesitantly asked, "Excuse me, is this 555-1758?"

A tearful reply said, "No, this is 555-1788."

"Oh, my, what a dreadful mistake," apologized the embarrassed voice on the phone. "I'm so terribly sorry. I must have dialed the wrong number."

Another brief pause before the would-be daughter asked, "Does this mean you're not coming over?"

# 75.
## The Graduation Gift

### Anonymous

A young man from a wealthy family was about to graduate from high school. It was the custom in his affluent neighborhood for the parents to give the graduate a car as a graduation present. Bill and his father spent months looking at cars, and the week before graduation they found the perfect one. Bill was certain that the car would be his on graduation night.

Imagine Bill's disappointment when, on the eve of his big day, his father handed him a gift-wrapped Bible! Bill was so angry, he hurled the Bible across his room and stormed out of the house, vowing never to return again. Bill and his father never saw each other again. Yet it was the news of his father's death that brought Bill back home again.

One night, as he sat going through his father's possessions that he was to inherit, Bill came across the Bible that his father had given him. He brushed away the dust and opened it to find a cashier's check, dated the day of his graduation— for the exact amount of the car they had chosen together.

## 76.
## From Parents to Children

### Anonymous

We gave you life, but we cannot live it for you.
We can teach you things, but we cannot make you learn.
We can give you directions, but we cannot be there to lead you.
We can allow you freedom, but we cannot account for it.
We can take you to church, but we cannot make you believe.
We can teach you right from wrong, but we cannot always decide for you.
We can offer you advice, but we cannot accept it for you.
We can give you love, but we cannot force it upon you.
We can teach you to share, but we cannot make you unselfish.
We can teach you respect, but we cannot force you to show honor.
We can advise you about friends, but we cannot choose them for you.
We can tell you about the facts of life, but we cannot build your reputation.
We can tell you about drinking, but we cannot say "no" for you.
We can tell you about lofty goals, but we cannot achieve them for you.
We can teach you about kindness, but we cannot force you to be gracious.

We can warn you about sin, but we cannot make you walk
    with God.
We can tell you how to live, but we cannot give you eternal
    life.

# 77.
## Lean on Me

### Brian Cavanaugh, T.O.R.

Every Olympic Games brings out examples of tremendous courage that capture the essence of the indomitable Olympic spirit. I remember the Barcelona 1992 Summer Games and one event that holds a special place in memory.

It was near the end of the men's four-hundred-meter race when Derrick Redmond of Great Britain suddenly crashed to the track clutching his right hamstring. Sprawled on the track, Redmond was writhing in pain as the other runners passed him. Inside himself he knew he that he had to get up—get up and finish the race. He struggled to his feet and began hopping awkwardly, dragging his injured leg, grimacing in pain.

Television viewers then saw, from the corner of their TV screens, an older man dash past security officials onto the track, running after Redmond. The man attempted to put his arm around the runner, but Redmond pushed him away. But the man continued along with Redmond until the excruciating pain overcame the runner and he slumped into the man's outstretched arms. The older man helped the runner up. That man was identified as Redmond's father, Jim. Father and son, arm in arm, continued down the track with the echoing applause supporting them to the finish line.

Jim Redmond supported his son throughout his athletic career and would not abandon Derrick in his moment of suffering. Five minutes after the race started, Derrick Redmond, supported by his father, crossed the finish line, four minutes and sixteen seconds *after* the gold medal winner.

Reporters swarmed over Jim Redmond for his comments after his son was helped off the track by the medical staff. The elder Redmond told the gathered press, "I'm more proud of my son than if he had won the race."

The Redmonds, father and son, exemplified the Olympic spirit as proclaimed by the founder of the modern Olympic Games, Baron de Coubertin, in 1896: "The most important thing in the Olympic Games is not to win, but to take part; just as the most important thing in life is not the triumph, but the struggle."


# 78.
## It Takes a Man

### Anonymous


It takes a man to be a father:

- to discipline his child through the inner life of the spirit rather than by the brute force of his hand;
- to listen and to share his time and energy even when he is weary or busy with his own interests;
- to be sensitive to his child's needs and pain rather than concerned with his own image and ego;
- to be able to admit a mistake or a failure and ask forgiveness and understanding;
- to be patient, honest, open, while acknowledging his own impatience, prejudices, frustrations and the anger and pain of knowing he is less than what he wants to be;
- to take his child into his arms with a loving embrace when broken relationships need to be healed;

- to love his child's spontaneity, just as he or she is, rather than demand predetermined and patterned responses;
- to celebrate with his child the spirit of God as they together find it in the beauty of dawn, the breeze caressing their faces, the exhilaration of running, the touch of a hand, the quiet glow of shared love;
- to see in the child the man or woman the child will become and be grateful for the opportunity to share in the growing up.

It takes a man to be himself—that he may be a father to his child, and that his child may be a child to him.

# 79.
## Novena of Las Posadas

### Anonymous

During the Advent season there is a Mexican-American celebration of *Posadas* that begins on December 16 and continues every night until December 24. This novena of Las Posadas commemorates Joseph and Mary's search for shelter in preparation of Mary's giving birth. During the nine nights of this festive celebration, "pilgrims" move about their neighborhood knocking on doors and seeking shelter. Given shelter, the neighbors then enjoy one another's company with parties.

The novena of Las Posadas is a good Advent tradition for each of us to reflect on. How hospitable are we to those who knock on our doors seeking *posadas* (shelter)? Do we pay attention to those who come to us seeking shelter for so many different reasons: food, housing, hurts, fear, worry, abuse, comfort, counsel, forgiveness? Are we hospitable to them, or must they seek shelter elsewhere?

There's a story[1] that illustrates this idea of *posadas*. A little child wandered through the streets of the town on a cold Christmas Eve, gazing at the busy people rushing back and forth, arms overflowing with presents. Everyone seemed happy. Everyone seemed to have a destination. Everyone, that is, except the little child.

As he walked, the bitter cold nipped at his cheeks and bit at his bare fingers. This was no night to be out alone. He must find shelter, a place to stay.

He turned down a broad boulevard dotted with large homes, the kind where yards are imprisoned by iron fences. Mustering his meager courage, he walked to the door of a very attractive house and peered through the curtains at the brightly decorated Christmas tree. Inside the house, children were playing, though they paused every now and then to shake a present that was under the tree.

The little child stretched on tiptoe and pushed the doorbell. Soon a tall boy opened the door slightly and looked down at the child. "I'm sorry," he said. "Our father is not home and he would not like a stranger to upset our Christmas Eve." The door closed slowly, almost apologetically.

The child shivered and went on to another home. This time a stout woman shouted at him, "Get off our property, and I mean now!"

The wind seemed as angry as the woman when the youngster reached the unsheltered sidewalk. He decided to try another street where the houses were a bit smaller, hoping people there would be more kindly. On this street he was greeted by a woman who was afraid he would bring germs into the house and a father who said there wasn't enough even for his own children. But mostly he was met with silence. People simply looked at him, shook their heads and quickly closed the door.

---

[1]Adapted from "A Legend for Christmas," in *Speaking in Stories,* ed. William R. White (Minneapolis: Augsburg Publishing House, 1982, p.55

"There must be some place in this town for me," the boy thought, as he stumbled along the dark streets. Now he was passing houses with fewer lights, houses much smaller in size. At the end of a nowhere street, the child stopped at a small, insignificant cottage with no curtains on the windows. It was easy to see into this tiny home. On a table sat a small Charlie Brown-type Christmas tree without lights. Near the fireplace a mother read to her two small children. Her daughter cuddled on her lap, while the son snuggled close to her feet.

"Mommy," the little girl cried out, interrupting the reading. "Someone, I think, is at the door."

"It's just the wind rustling the trees," her brother assured her.

But before the mother could continue, the noise was heard again, and the three of them rushed to the door to see what had made the sound. There in the doorway stood the little child, shivering in the cold.

The mother scooped up the child and pressed him tightly to her as she carried him to the living room. "Quickly, warm some milk," she called to her son as she began rubbing the child's numbed fingers between her warm hands. Pushing back his tangled hair, she tenderly kissed the child on the forehead and whispered, "We are delighted that you have come to share our Christmas with us."

For nearly an hour the four huddled around the fireplace until feeling began to return to the frozen body of the little stranger. When their guest seemed to be warmed, the little girl said, "Finish the story, Mommy," The mother went back to her place on the couch and opened the book to her bookmark.

Suddenly a powerful light flooded the room. The small family turned to see the little stranger transform before their eyes. The light from his face shone so bright that they were forced to turn their heads. Then the light darted out of the house and, as the family rushed to the door, they watched the beam of light ascend until all that was visible was a star that shone brilliantly over their home, bathing the entire area in radiant light.

The boy was the first to break the silence. He asked, "Mother, was that the Christ Child?"

"I think so," she said simply.

It is said that each Christmas God sends his Son wandering the streets of some town in our land, seeking a place of shelter, a *posadas*, in which to be welcomed and warmed. When he is accepted, God sends a star of brilliant light to shine. This Christmas, be attentive and look around you for those in need. Look up, then, and see if God's sign shines over your house.

## 80.
## Time to Get Off Your Knees

### Anonymous

Shrieking in the middle of the night, the smoke detector startled the family awake. Immediately jumping from their bed, the parents yelled for their children to hurry out of the house. Once outside, the parents started counting and discovered that one child was missing. A parent's worst fear was now realized. Then they saw their son at a second floor window, trapped by the flames.

The father, a devout church elder, immediately dropped to his knees, praying that God would somehow work to save his son. The mother, too, was a person of deep faith, but also a very practical woman. Immediately, she ran next door, yanked a neighbor's extension ladder from the garage wall, propped it against her house and rescued her son from the flaming house.

There are times when the best way to express faith is to get off your knees, go get a ladder and do what needs to be done in a given situation.

# 81.
## The Finishing Touch

### Anonymous

Phidias very likely was the greatest sculptor among the ancient Greeks. Legend tells us that he was extremely careful when applying the finishing touches to the beautiful statue of Diana, which was to adorn the Acropolis in Athens. As he applied his chisel to the back side of Diana's head, he shaped each strand of hair with great patience, giving his full attention to the tiniest detail.

An observer reminded Phidias that the statue would stand one hundred feet high with its back to a huge marble wall. "Why waste your time on those finishing touches that will never be seen?" he asked. "Who will ever know of such detailed work in the back?"

Phidias solemnly replied, "I will know!"

# 82.
## Envy's Clutching Power

### Anonymous

A couple, vacationing in Maine, visited the harbor to watch the boats return from fishing and trapping lobsters. One lobster boat docked near where they sat and unloaded buckets of freshly trapped lobsters. The wife became intrigued as she watched the lobsters scurry about in a bucket. She noticed that as soon as one lobster began to climb its way out of the pail, the other lobsters would pull it back down. It seemed to her that it would have been fairly easy for each lobster to crawl out of the bucket, except that they always were being pulled back down by the others.

Lobsters certainly can teach us about the powerful effects of envy in human nature as well. Doesn't it seem that as soon as one person decides to stretch and climb out of the "bucket," there are so many others clutching to pull him or her back down? Rather, shouldn't we try to support and push the other person farther along?

# 83.
# Vying for the Crown of Thorns

## Anonymous

Wendy Kaminer is the author of the best-selling book *I'm Dysfunctional, You're Dysfunctional,* a critical look at our national obsession with the "cult of victimization."

In an interview in *The Door* magazine Ms. Kaminer says, "There is something very mean-spirited about this 'cult of victimization.' For all the talk about caring and sharing, it is an excuse for people not to have any compassion." Ms. Kaminer continues, "The payoff of claiming that you are a victim is that you always get to put your problems first. Primarily, this self-help movement is a movement of the middle class, and it reflects what is called compassion fatigue. It's middle-class people saying, 'I'm tired of hearing about those poor children of poverty....about the problem of minorities in this country. I have problems, too. My father wasn't nice to me.' It is as if people are saying, 'Me too, me too.' Everyone is vying for the crown of thorns."

If we are faithful to Christ's call to discipleship, we are to put aside our own sense of victimization for the sake of others. In letting go of ourselves, in putting ourselves at the service of others, in seeking justice and peace and healing for them, we can bring the resurrection into both our lives and theirs.

## 84.
## The Devil and the Harvest

### Anonymous

There's an old European story about a traveler who came upon a barn where the devil had stored seeds that he planned to sow in the hearts of people. There were bags of seeds variously marked "Hatred," "Fear," "Lust," "Despair," "Unforgiveness," "Envy," "Greed," "Drunkenness."

Out from the shadows, the devil appeared and struck up a conversation with the traveler. He gleefully told the traveler how easily the seeds sprouted in the hearts of men and women everywhere.

"Tell me," the traveler asked, "are there any hearts in which these seeds will not sprout?"

Glancing about carefully, the devil slyly confessed, "These seeds will never sprout in the heart of a kind, generous, thankful and joy-filled person.

## 85.
## If

### Rudyard Kipling

If you can keep your head when all about you
    Are losing theirs and blaming it on you,
If you can trust yourself when all men doubt you,
    But make allowance for their doubting too;
If you can wait and not be tired by waiting,
    Or being lied about, don't deal in lies,
Or being hated, don't give way to hating,
    And yet don't look too good, nor talk too wise:

If you can dream—and not make dreams your master;
  If you can think—and not make thoughts your aim;
If you can meet with Triumph and Disaster
  And treat those two imposters just the same;
If you can bear to hear the truth you've spoken
  Twisted by knaves to make a trap for fools,
Or watch the things you gave your life to, broken,
  And stoop and build 'em up with worn-out tools:

If you can make one heap of all your winnings
  And risk it on one turn of pitch-and-toss,
And lose, and start again at your beginnings
  And never breathe a word about your loss;
If you can force your heart and nerve and sinew
  To serve your turn long after they are gone,
And so hold on when there is nothing in you
  Except the Will which says to them: "Hold on!"

If you can talk with crowds and keep your virtue,
  Or walk with kings—nor lose the common touch,
If neither foes nor loving friends can hurt you,
  If all men count with you, but none too much;
If you can fill the unforgiving minute
  With sixty seconds' worth of distance run,
Yours is the Earth and everything that's in it,
  And—which is more—you'll be a Man, my son!

Written in 1910 for his twelve-year-old son, John.


## 86.
## Looking for Forgiveness

### Anonymous


There's a Spanish tale of a father and son who had
become estranged after years of bitter strife. The son finally

ran away. Finding that his son was missing, the father became heartbroken and set off to find him. He searched for months to no avail. Finally, in a last desperate effort, the father placed an ad in the city newspaper. The ad read:

Dear Paco,
Meet me in front of the bell tower in the plaza at noon on Saturday. All is forgiven.
I love you.

Your Father.

That Saturday eight hundred Pacos—men and boys—showed up in the plaza, looking for forgiveness and love from their fathers.

# 87.
## The Three *Ups*

### Jeff MacNelly

Several years back, there was a terrific scene in Jeff Mac-Nelly's comic strip "Shoe." The main character is a frazzled "Perfesser" sitting in his usual spot in Roz's Diner. He seems hard at work on his latest writing.

Roz stands behind the counter and asks the "Perfesser" what he's writing this time. "I'm writing the definitive self-help book based on my personal philosophy," he explains.

"Your philosophy?" Roz chuckles.

The "Perfesser" indignantly looks up and says, "Yes. I'm calling my book *The Three Ups: Shut Up, Grow Up and Listen Up.*"

# 88.
# Five Lessons from Geese

## Tom J. Watson

Tom J. Watson presented, years ago, an interesting paradigm based on observing geese flying in formation. He developed five lessons from his observation that served him well over the years.

As each bird flaps its wings, it creates an "uplift" for the bird following. By flying in a "V-shaped" formation, the whole flock adds 71 percent greater flying range than if each bird flew alone.

> Lesson 1: People who share a common direction and sense of community can get where they are going quicker and easier because they are traveling on the thrust of one another.

Whenever a goose falls out of formation, it suddenly feels the drag and resistance of trying to fly alone, and quickly gets back into formation to take advantage of the "lifting power" of the bird immediately in front.

> Lesson 2: If we have as much sense as a goose, we will stay in formation with those who are headed where we want to go and be willing to accept their help, as well as give of ourselves to others.

When the lead goose gets tired, it rotates back into formation and another goose flies at the point position.

> Lesson 3: It pays to take turns doing the hard tasks, sharing leadership and responsibility. People, like geese, are interdependent on each other.

The geese in formation honk from behind to encourage those up front to keep up speed.

Lesson 4:   We need to make sure our honking from behind is encouraging, and not something else.

When a goose gets sick, or wounded, or shot down, other geese seem to drop out of formation to follow it down and help protect it. They stay close until the goose is able to fly again or dies. Then they launch out on their journey with another formation or catch up with the flock.

Lesson 5:   If we have as much sense as geese, we, too, will *stand by one another* in difficult times, as well as when we are strongest.

## 89.
## The Easter Pageant

### Anonymous

The school was getting ready for the annual Easter pageant. All the children who were participating were asked to choose which part they would want to play. Suzy chose Mary Magdalene; Sammy and Johnny, together, wanted to be the donkey; and so forth.

The teachers were amused as they watched the enthusiasm of the children grow as each part was assigned. When it came time for Jimmy's turn to choose, there were not many roles left, but he happily wanted to be the huge rock that sealed the tomb.

After the pageant was over and Jimmy was going home with his parents, his mother expressed how let down they were that he didn't have a larger, more prominent role in the play.

Jimmy, however, was bouncing excitedly all over the back seat, obviously thrilled with his performance in the pageant.

Finally his mom turned to him and asked, "Tell me, Jimmy, why are you so happy about being the rock to the tomb? Wouldn't you have liked to have a bigger part to play?"

Jimmy replied quite innocently, "Oh, no, Mom, just think! I'm the one who gets to let Jesus out! What could be better?"

# 90.
## One of God's Children

### Anonymous

One winter day, a little boy was standing on a grate next to a bakery, trying to keep his shoeless feet warm. A woman passing by saw the frosty-toed child and her heart ached. He had on only a lightweight jacket and no shoes, and the air was chilly, the wind sharp.

"Where are your shoes, young man?" she asked. The boy reluctantly admitted he didn't have any. "Why don't you come with me and we'll see what we can do about that?" the woman said. Taking his hand, she led him into a nearby department store and bought him a new pair of shoes and a warm jacket.

When they came back out onto the street, the little boy was so excited that he immediately started to run off to show his family his gifts. Suddenly he halted, turned around and ran back to the woman. He thanked her and then hesitated, "Ma'am, could I ask you a question? Ma'am, are you God's wife?"

The woman smiled and said, "Oh, no, I'm not God's wife, just one of God's children."

The little boy grinned and nodded enthusiastically, "I knew it! I just knew you were related!"

# 91.
## Tips for Parent-Teen Relationships

### Anonymous

1. Do not forget to pat them on the back. The teen years are doing and going years. Show interest in what is happening. Spend more time encouraging the good than punishing the bad.
2. Give them time to be alone. This is often good tonic, for it gives them time to think things through. Respect their wish for privacy.
3. Keep the lines of communication open. Maybe teens do not even understand themselves, but they want parents to whom they can go, and who they can be sure will at least listen and let them explain.
4. Keep learning. Young people expect you to know. If you do not, find out real soon!
5. Stand by them, not over them. Show quiet concern for what teens wear and where they go. Prepare them to lead their lives, not yours. Stand by. Teens want guidance, but not nagging about every little thing.


# 92.
## Twenty-One Words to Change Your Life

### Anonymous

In the spring of 1871, a young man picked up a book and read twenty-one words that had a profound effect on his future. A medical student, he was worried about passing a final examination, worried about what to do, where to go, how to build up a practice, how to make a living.

The twenty-one words that this young med student read helped him to become the most famous physician of his generation. He was even knighted by the king of England. When he died, two huge volumes containing 1,466 pages were required to tell the story of his life.

His name was Sir William Osler. Here are the twenty-one words that he read—twenty-one words from Thomas Carlyle that helped him lead a life free from worry: *Our main business is not to see what lies dimly at a distance, but to do what lies clearly at hand.*

The load of tomorrow, added to that of yesterday, carried today, makes the strongest falter. Shut off the future as tightly as the past. The future is today; there is no tomorrow....Waste of energy, mental distress, nervous worries, all dog the steps of a person who is anxious about the future. The best possible way to prepare for tomorrow is to concentrate with all your intelligence, all your enthusiasm on doing today's work superbly today. That is the only possible way you can prepare for the future.

# 93.
## The Tent of Refuge

## Walter J. Burghardt, S.J.

In the Hashemite Kingdom of Jordan, two Bedouin youths got into a fight, tumbling to the ground in their fury. One boy pulled out a knife, plunging it fatally into the other's chest. In fear he fled across the desert, fled from the slain boy's vengeance-seeking relatives, fled to find a Bedouin sanctuary, a "tent of refuge," designed by law for those who kill unintentionally or in the heat of anger.

At last he reached what might be a refuge—the black-tented encampment of a nomad tribe. The boy flung himself at the feet of the leader, an aged sheik, and begged him: "I have killed in the heat of anger; I implore your protection. I seek the refuge of your tent."

"If God wills," the old man responded, "I grant it to you, as long as you remain with us."

A few days later the avenging relatives tracked the fugitive to the encampment. They described the assailant to the sheik and asked, "Have you seen this man? Is he here? For we will have him."

"He is here," said the sheik, "but you will not have him."

"But he has killed, and we, the blood relatives of the slain boy, will stone him according to the law."

The sheik raised his voice, "You will not, as long as he remains with us."

"We demand him," the relatives declared.

"No! The boy has my protection," said the sheik. "I've given my word, my promise of refuge."

"But you don't understand," the relatives implored. "He killed your grandson!"

The old man was silent. No one dared to speak. Then, in visible anguish, with tears searing his face, the old man stood up and spoke ever so slowly, "My only grandson—he is dead?"

"Yes, your only grandson is dead."

"Then...," said the sheik, "then this boy will be my grandson. He is forgiven, and he will live with us as my own. Go now; it is finished."

# 94.
# The Old Beach Lady

## Anonymous

It was the first time the family had saved up enough money to rent a cottage at the beach. After unpacking and somewhat arranging things, they all picked up their towels and blankets and went to the beach. The children were running in and out of the surf and building sand castles when, in the distance, a stooped-over old woman appeared. Her scraggily gray hair was blowing in the wind and her clothes were dirty and ragged. She was muttering something incoherent to herself as she picked up things from the beach and put them into a plastic bag.

The parents quickly called their children to their side and told them to stay away from that old lady. As she passed by, bending down every now and then to pick up things, she smiled at the family. But her greeting wasn't returned.

It was later on that a longtime resident of the beach community told them that the little old lady had a son who, years ago, once cut his foot on the sand and it later became severely infected. Since then she made it her lifelong crusade to pick up bits of glass and cans from the beach so that children would not cut their feet.

## 95.
## Excellence Is No Trifle

### Anonymous

A friend once called on Michelangelo just as he was putting the finishing touches on one of his great works of art. Sometime later the same friend again visited the great artist, and, to his astonishment, found Michelangelo still at work on the same piece of sculpture, but with no obvious improvement as far as he could tell.

"Have you been away since I saw you last?" the friend asked Michelangelo.

"By no means," said the artist. "I've been retouching

this part, polishing that, softening this feature and strengthening that muscle—and so on."

"But," said the visitor, "these are only trifles that don't matter."

"That may be," replied the artist, "but bear in mind that trifles make excellence, and excellence is no trifle."


# 96.
# Have I Misdirected Others?

## Anonymous

As an old man was lying on his deathbed, it was clear to his pastor that something was troubling him. Finally, the old man broke the silence: "When I was a youngster," he said, "I played a prank that haunts me to this day. One day I twisted the highway route signs in opposite directions so the arrows would direct travelers in the wrong direction.

"I wonder, as I lie here now, how many people I misdirected by that action—and, I wonder, how many I misdirected by the actions of my life."


# 97.
# A Child's Advice to His Parents

## Anonymous

My hands are small. Please don't expect perfection whenever I make a bed, draw a picture, or throw a ball.

My eyes have not seen the world as yours have. Please let me explore it at my own level without unnecessary restrictions.

Housework will always be there, but I will be little only for a short time. Please take time to explain about this wonderful world.

My feelings are tender. Please be sensitive to my needs. Treat me as you would like to be treated.

I am a special gift from God. Treasure me as God intended, holding me accountable for my actions, giving me guidelines to live by and disciplining me in a loving manner.

I need your encouragement to grow, so go easy on the criticism. Try to correct my behavior without criticizing me as a person.

Give me the freedom to make decisions. Permit me to fail so I can learn from my mistakes. Then I'll be prepared to make the kind of decisions life requires of me as an adult.

Don't do jobs over that I have done. This makes me feel that my efforts don't quite measure up to your expectations. I know it's hard, but please don't compare me with my brother or sister.

Please don't be afraid to leave for a weekend together. Kids need vacations from parents, just as parents need to get away occasionally. This is also a great way to show us kids that your marriage is very special.

Please set a good example by taking me to church and religious education class regularly. I enjoy learning more about God.

# 98.
# My Child, What Can I Give You?

## Lydia Lightner

I should like to give you everything so that you lack for nothing, not even one single desire, but I know that from want of many things I have come to be satisfied with what I have and to think of others and their needs.

I should like to give you a life full of fun and games, but I know that because of the many "chores" and responsibilities of my youth, I have learned to be responsible.

I should like to protect you from all the errors of your youth, but I know that because of my failures, I have learned to make better decisions.

I should like to give you a profession or wealth or importance, but I realize that man is truly happy only when he fulfills the purpose for which God created him. What then, my child, can I give you that would be of any real value?

I give you my love, which means that I accept you, without reservations, just as you are and will be.

I give you my personal presence in order that you will have the security you need during your childhood.

I give you my ears, in the sense that I will never be too busy to listen to you—sometimes never uttering even one word.

I give you opportunities to work so that you might learn to do it without shame and come to enjoy the satisfaction of work well done.

I give you my counsel only when it is necessary or you ask for it, so that you might avoid some of the mistakes I have made.

I give you my consolation when you have failed or feel discouraged, but I will not always protect you from the consequences of your sins.

I give you instruction in the way of the Lord so that when you are older, you will never depart from it.

I give you my daily prayers that the Lord will keep you and guide you in such a way that you, my child, will be someone who will serve and glorify our heavenly Father.

This I give you with all my love.

Your Mother

# 99.
# Add a Shimmering Quality

## Anonymous

The French painter Georges Seurat's technique—Pointillism, or Neo-Impressionism—was painstaking. He used tiny, detached strokes of pure color, a multitude of colorful dots. Gazed at up close, these are so small as not to be distinguished as part of a design, but together they make one grand composition. Those tiny dots of color, seen alongside other dots of differing tones—red, blue, yellow or their complements—suggest outlines and shapes of things.

Art critics say those tiny dots add a shimmering quality of light to the painting; all make their own special kind of order. Seurat believed that one dot of color placed close to another suggested to the eye of the viewer still another color; they also suggested varied shapes and figures. The colors are not in the individual dots but result from their relation to the many other dots.

Is not a community, a team, a parish made up of little and varied dots of faith and love? Each one of us is of a different color and shape, and each carries one's own quality of light. When these individual talents are free to be what they are, to reflect their own true color, to stand by but in concert with the differing talents of others, they can shimmer together; they can set up the patterns and outlines of teamwork, of cooperation and of community.

# 100.
# Prepare for Service to God

## Martin Buber

Martin Buber tells the story about a rabbi's disciple who begged his master to teach him how to prepare his soul for the service of God. The holy man told him to go to Rabbi Abraham, who, at the time, was still an innkeeper.

The disciple did as instructed and lived in the inn for several weeks without observing any vestige of holiness in the innkeeper, who, from Morning Prayer till night, devoted himself to the affairs of his business. Finally, the disciple approached him and asked him what he did all day.

"My most important occupation," said Rabbi Abraham, "is to clean the dishes properly, so that not the slightest trace of food is left, and to clean and dry the pots and pans, so that they do not rust."

When the disciple returned home and reported to his rabbi what he had seen and heard, the rabbi said to him, "Now you know the answer about how to prepare your soul for the service of God."

The way to reach God is by doing *everything* wholeheartedly and genuinely; everything (and every act) is full of God's holiness—so treat it accordingly with dignity and respect.

# Source Acknowledgments

This book is the fruition of years of reading, listening and transcribing stories from many and varied sources. I thank the authors and publishers who have given their generous cooperation and permission to include these stories in this collection. Further reproduction without permission is prohibited.

Every effort has been made to acknowledge the proper source for each story; regrettably, I am unable to give proper credit to every story. When the proper source becomes known, proper credit will be given in future editions of this book.

1. GIVEN UP HOPE UNTIL...
   Anonymous
   Source Unknown

2. THE NOBLEST SOLUTION
   Anonymous
   Source Unknown

3. TO HAVE A GREAT THEME (ADAPTED)
   Harry Huxhold
   *Emphasis,* Vol. 22, No. 3

4. THE TROUBLE TREE
   Anonymous
   Source Unknown

5. A SMILE AS WARM AS THE SUN
   Beth Schoentrup
   *Catholic Digest,* June 1993, p. 144
   Used with author's permission

# Storytelling Reading List

Abrahams, Roger D., ed. *African Folktales: Traditional Stories of the Black World*. NY: Pantheon Books-Random House, 1983.

*Aesop's Fables*. London: Bracken Books, 1986.

Afasas'ev, Aleksandr, ed. *Russian Fairy Tales*. NY: Pantheon Books-Random House.

Allison, Christine, ed. *Teach Your Children Well*. NY: Bantam-Delacorte Press, 1993.

Arcodia, Charles. *Stories for Sharing*. Newtown, Australia: E. J. Dwyer, Ltd., 1991.

Armstrong, David. *Managing by Storying Around: A New Method of Leadership*. NY: Doubleday Currency Book, 1992.

Aurelio, John. *Story Sunday*. NY: Paulist Press, 1978.

———. *Fables for God's People*. NY: Crossroad, 1988.

———. *Colors! Stories of the Kingdom*. NY: Crossroad, 1993.

Ausubel, Nathan, ed. *A Treasury of Jewish Folklore*. NY: Crown Publishers, 1948.

Baldock, John. *The Little Book of Sufi Wisdom*. Rockport, MA: Element Books, 1995.

Bausch, William. *Storytelling: Imagination and Faith*. Mystic, CT: Twenty-Third Publications, 1984.

———. *A World of Stories for Preachers and Teachers*. Mystic, CT: Twenty-Third Publications, 1998.

Benjamin, Don-Paul, and Ron Miner. *Come Sit with Me Again: Sermons for Children*. NY: The Pilgrim Press, 1987.

Bennett, William J., ed. *The Book of Virtues: A Treasury of Great Moral Stories*. NY: Simon and Schuster, 1993.

————. *The Moral Compass: Stories for a Life's Journey.* NY: Simon and Schuster, 1995.

Bettelheim, Bruno. *The Uses of Enchantment.* NY: Vintage Books, 1977.

Bleefeld, Rabbi Bradley R., and Robert L. Shook. *Saving the World Entire: And 100 Other Beloved Parables from the Talmud.* NY: Penguin Putnam/Plume, 1998.

Bodo, Murray, O.F.M., *Tales of St. Francis: Ancient Stories for Contemporary Living.* NY: Doubleday, 1988.

Bradt, Kevin M., S.J. *Story as a Way of Knowing.* Kansas City: Sheed and Ward, 1997.

Briggs, Katharine. *An Encyclopedia of Fairies.* NY: Pantheon Books-Random House, 1976.

Bruchac, Joseph, and Michael J. Caduto. *Native American Stories.* Golden, CO: Fulcrum Publishing, 1991.

Buber, Martin. *Tales of the Hasidim: Early Masters.* NY: Schocken Books, 1975.

————. *Tales of the Hasidim: Later Masters.* NY: Schocken Books, 1948.

Bushnaq, Inea, ed. *Arab Folktales.* NY: Pantheon Books-Random House, 1986.

Calvino, Italo, ed. *Italian Folktales.* NY: Pantheon Books-Random House, 1980.

Canfield, Jack, and Mark V. Hansen. *Chicken Soup for the Soul.* Deerfield Beach, FL: Health Communications, Inc., 1993.

————. *A 2nd Helping of Chicken Soup for the Soul.* Deerfield Beach, FL: Health Communications, Inc., 1995.

————. *A 3rd Helping of Chicken Soup for the Soul.* Deerfield Beach, FL: Health Communications, Inc., 1996.

Canfield, Jack, Mark V. Hansen and Barry Spilchuk. *A Cup of Chicken Soup for the Soul.* Deerfield Beach, FL: Health Communications, Inc., 1996.

Canfield, Jack, Mark V. Hansen, Jennifer Read Hawthorne and Marci Shimoff. *A Cup of Chicken Soup for the*

*Woman's Soul.* Deerfield Beach, FL: Health Communications, Inc., 1996.

Canfield, Jack, Mark V. Hansen and Patty Hansen. *Condensed Chicken Soup for the Soul.* Deerfield Beach, FL: Health Communications, Inc., 1996.

Canfield, Jack, Mark V. Hansen, Patty Aubery and Nancy Mitchell. *Chicken Soup for the Christian Soul.* Deerfield Beach, FL: Health Communications, Inc., 1997.

Canfield, Jack, Mark V. Hansen and Kimberly Kirberger. *Chicken Soup for the Teenage Soul.* Deerfield Beach, FL: Health Communications, Inc., 1997.

Canfield, Jack, Mark V. Hansen, Hanoch McCarty and Meladee McCarty. *A 4th Course of Chicken Soup for the Soul.* Deerfield Beach, FL: Health Communications, Inc., 1997.

Carroll, James. *Wonder and Worship.* NY: Newman Press, 1970.

Cassady, Marsh. *Storytelling: Step by Step.* San Jose, CA: Resource Publications, 1990.

————. *The Art of Storytelling: Creative Ideas for Preparation and Performance.* Colorado Springs: Meriwether Publishing Ltd., 1994.

Castagnola, Larry, S.J. *More Parables for Little People.* San Jose, CA: Resource Publications, Inc, 1987.

Cattan, Henry. *The Garden of Joys: An Anthology of Oriental Anecdotes, Fables and Proverbs.* London: Namara Publications, Ltd., 1979.

Cavanaugh, Brian, T.O.R. *The Sower's Seeds: One Hundred Inspiring Stories for Preaching, Teaching and Public Speaking.* Mahwah, NJ: Paulist Press, 1990.

————. *More Sower's Seeds: Second Planting.* Mahwah, NJ: Paulist Press, 1992.

————. *Fresh Packet of Sower's Seeds: Third Planting.* Mahwah, NJ: Paulist Press, 1994.

————. *Sower's Seeds Aplenty: Fourth Planting.* Mahwah, NJ: Paulist Press, 1996.

————. *Sower's Seeds of Virtue: Stories of Faith, Hope and Love*. Mahwah, NJ: Paulist Press, 1997.

————. *Sower's Seeds of Encouragement: 100 Stories of Hope, Humor and Healing*. Mahwah, NJ: Paulist Press, 1998.

Chalk, Gary. *Tales of Ancient China*. London: Frederick Muller, 1984.

Chapman, H. S., ed. *1001 One-Minute Stories*. Boston: Perry Mason Co., 1927.

Chappell, Stephen, O.S.B *Dragons and Demons, Angels and Eagles: Morality Tales for Teens*. St. Louis: Liguori Publications, 1990.

Charlton, James, and Barbara Gilson, eds. *A Christmas Treasury of Yuletide Stories and Poems*. NY: Galahad Books-LDAP, 1992.

Chinnen, Allan B., M.D. *Once Upon a Midlife*. NY: Jeremy P. Tarcher-Putnam Books, 1992.

————. *Beyond the Hero*. NY: Jeremy P. Tarcher-Putnam Books, 1993.

Colainni, James F., Sr., ed. *Sunday Sermons Treasury of Illustrations*. Pleasantville, NJ: Voicings Publications, 1982.

Colainni, James F., Jr., ed. *Contemporary Sermon Illustrations*. Ventnor, NJ: Italicus, Inc., 1991.

Colum, Padraic, ed. *A Treasury of Irish Folklore*. 2nd ed. NY: Crown Publishers, Inc., 1967.

*Complete Grimm's Fairy Tales, The*. NY: Pantheon Books, 1972.

*Contemporary Chinese Tales*. Beijing: Panda Books-Chinese Literature Press, 1990.

Cornils, Stanley, ed. *34 Two-Minute Talks for Youth and Adults*. Cincinnati, OH: Standard Publications, 1985.

Curtin, Jeremiah, ed. *Myths and Folk Tales of Ireland*. NY: Dover, 1975.

Dasent, George Webbe, ed. *East O' the Sun and West O' the Moon*. NY: Dover, 1970.

De La Fontaine, Jean, ed. *Selected Fables*. NY: Dover, 1968.

de Mello, Anthony, S.J. *The Song of the Bird*. India: Gujarat Sahitya Prakash, 1982.

———. *One Minute Wisdom*. NY: Doubleday and Co., 1986.

———. *Taking Flight*. NY: Doubleday, 1988.

———. *The Heart of the Enlightened*. NY: Doubleday, 1989.

———. *One Minute Nonsense*. Chicago: Loyola University Press, 1992.

———. *More One Minute Nonsense*. Chicago: Loyola University Press, 1993.

de Voragine, Jacobus. *The Golden Legend: Reading on the Saints, Volume 1*. Princeton, NJ: Princeton University Press, 1993.

———. *The Golden Legend: Reading on the Saints, Volume 2*. Princeton, NJ: Princeton University Press, 1993.

Doleski, Teddi. *The Hurt*. Mahwah, NJ: Paulist Press, 1983.

Dosick, Wayne. *Golden Rules: The Ten Ethical Values Parents Need to Teach Their Children*. San Francisco: Harper-Collins, 1995.

Erdoes, Richard, and Alfonso Ortiz, eds. *American Indian Myths and Legends*. NY: Pantheon Books-Random House, 1984.

Evans, Ivor, ed. *Brewer's Dictionary of Phrase and Fable*. 14th ed. NY: Harper and Row, 1989.

Fahy, Mary. *The Tree That Survived the Winter*. Mahwah, NJ: Paulist Press, 1989.

Farra, Harry. *The Little Monk*. Mahwah, NJ: Paulist Press, 1994.

Feehan, James A. *Story Power!: Compelling Illustrations for Preaching and Teaching*. (Originally published as *Stories for Preachers*. Dublin: Mercier Press, 1988.) San Jose, CA: Resource Publications, 1994.

Forest, Heather. *Wisdom Tales from Around the World*. Little Rock, AR: August House, 1996.

Frankel, Ellen. *The Classic Tales: 4,000 years of Jewish Lore*. Northvale, NJ: Jason Aronson, 1989.

Gallehugh, Sue, Ph.D., and Allen Gallehugh. *Bedtime Stories for Grown-Ups: Fairy Tale Psychology.* Deerfield Beach, FL: Health Communications, Inc., 1995.

Giono, Jean. *The Man Who Planted Trees.* VT: Chelsea Green Publishing Co., 1985.

Glassie, Henry, ed. *Irish Folk Tales.* NY: Pantheon Books-Random House, 1985.

Graves, Alfred. *The Irish Fairy Book.* NY: Greenwich House, 1983.

Greer, Colin, and Herbert Kohl, eds. *A Call to Character.* NY: HarperCollins, 1995.

Harris, Joel Chandler. *The Complete Tales of Uncle Remus.* Comp. Richard Chase. Boston: Houghton Mifflin, 1983 (1955).

Hasler, Richard A. *God's Game Plan: Sports Anecdotes for Preachers.* Lima, OH: C.S.S. Publishing Company, Inc., 1990.

Haugaard, Erik Christian, trans. *Hans Christian Anderson: The Complete Fairy Tales and Stories.* NY: Anchor-Doubleday, 1974.

Haviland, Virginia, ed. *North American Legends.* NY: Philomel Books, 1979.

Hays, Edward. *Twelve and One-Half Keys.* Leavenworth, KS: Forest of Peace Books, 1981.

―――. *Sundancer: A Mystical Fantasy.* Leavenworth, KS: Forest of Peace Books, 1982.

―――. *The Ethiopian Tattoo Shop.* Leavenworth, KS: Forest of Peace Books, 1983.

―――. *A Pilgrim's Almanac: Reflections for Each Day of the Year.* Leavenworth, KS: Forest of Peace Books, Inc., 1989.

―――. *The Magic Lantern.* Leavenworth, KS: Forest of Peace Books, 1991.

―――. *The Christmas Eve Storyteller.* Leavenworth, KS: Forest of Peace Books, 1992.

―――. *Holy Fools and Mad Hatters.* Leavenworth, KS: Forest of Peace Books, 1993.

—————. *The Quest for the Flaming Pearl*. Leavenworth, KS: Forest of Peace Books, 1994.

—————. *The Old Hermit's Almanac: Daily Meditations for the Journey of Life*. Leavenworth, KS: Forest of Peace Books, 1997.

Henderschedt, James L. *The Magic Stone*. San Jose, CA: Resource Publications, Inc. (160 E. Virginia Street, S-290), 1988.

—————. *The Topsy-Turvy Kingdom*. San Jose, CA: Resource Publications, Inc. (160 E. Virginia Street, S- 290), 1990.

—————. *The Light in the Lantern*. San Jose, CA: Resource Publications, Inc. (160 E. Virginia Street, S- 290), 1991.

—————. *The Beggar's Bowl: Parables and Short Stories for Spiritual Preaching*. Bethlehem, PA: Faith Journey Creations (PO Box 4219), 1994.

—————. *The Hammer Man*. Bethlehem, PA: Faith Journey Creations (PO Box 4219), 1995.

Holdcraft, Paul E., ed. *Snappy Stories for Sermons and Speeches*. Nashville: Abingdon Press, 1987.

Holt, David, and Bill Mooney. *Ready-to-Tell Tales*. Little Rock, AR: August House, 1994.

Hughes, R. Kent. *1001 Great Stories & Quotes*. Wheaton, IL: Tyndale House, 1998.

Jaffe, Nina, and Steve Zeitlin, eds. *While Standing on One Foot: Puzzle Stories and Wisdom Tales from the Jewish Tradition*. NY: Henry Holt, 1993.

James, Cheewa. *Catch the Whisper of the Wind: Inspirational Stories and Proverbs from Native Americans*. Deerfield Beach, FL: Health Communications, Inc., 1995.

Johnson, Miriam. *Inside Twenty-Five Classic Children's Stories*. Mahwah, NJ: Paulist Press, 1986.

Juknialis, Joseph. *Winter Dreams and other such friendly dragons*. San Jose, CA: Resource Publications, Inc., 1979.

Kronberg, Ruthilde, and Patricia C. McKissack. *A Piece of the*

*Wind and Other Stories to Tell*. NY: Harper and Row, 1990.

———. *Clever Folk: Tales of Wisdom, Wit and Wonder*. Englewood, CO: Libraries Unlimited, Inc., 1993.

Kurtz, Ernest and Katherine Ketchman. *The Spirituality of Imperfection: Storytelling and the Journey to Wholeness*. NY: Bantam, 1992.

Lang, Andrew, ed. *The Brown Fairy Book*. NY: Dover, 1965.

Laz, Medard. *Love Adds a Little Chocolate*. Ann Arbor, MI: Servant Publications, 1997.

L'Estrange, Sir Rodger. *Fables of Aesop*. Drawings by Alexander Calder. NY: Dover Publications, 1967.

Levin, Meyer. *Classic Hasidic Tales*. NY: Dorset Press, 1985.

Levine, David, ed. *The Fables of Aesop*. NY: Dorset Press, 1989.

Lewis, Naomi, ed. *Cry Wolf and Other Aesop Fables*. NY: Oxford University Press, 1988.

Lieberman, Leo and Arthur Beringause. *Classics of Jewish Literature*. Secaucus, NJ: Book Sales, Inc., 1988.

Litherland, Janet. *Storytelling from the Bible*. Colorado Springs, CO: Meriwhether Publishing Ltd., 1991.

Livo, Norma J., and Sandra A. Rietz. *Storytelling: Process and Practice*. Littleton, CO: Libraries Unlimited, Inc., 1986.

———. *Storytelling Folklore Sourcebook*. Littleton, CO: Libraries Unlimited, Inc., 1991.

Lobel, Arnold. *Fables*. NY: Harper Collins, 1980.

Loder, Ted. *Tracks in the Snow: Tales Spun from the Manger*. San Diego, CA: LuraMedia, 1985.

Lufburrow, Bill. *Illustrations Without Sermons*. Nashville: Abingdon Press, 1985.

MacDonald, Margaret Read. *Peace Tales: World Folktales to Talk About*. Hamden, CT: Linnet Books, 1992.

———. *The Storyteller's Start-Up Book: Finding, Learning, Performing and Using Folktales*. Little Rock, AR: August House, 1993.

*The Magic Ox and Other Tales of the Effendi.* Beijing: Foreign Languages Press, 1986.

Marbach, Ethel. *The White Rabbit: A Franciscan Christmas Story.* Cincinnati, OH: St. Anthony Messenger Press, 1984.

Martin, Rafe, ed. *The Hungry Tigress: Buddhist Legends and Jataka Tales.* Berkeley, CA: Parallax Press, 1990.

McArdle, Jack. *150 Stories for Preachers and Teachers.* Mystic, CT: Twenty-Third Publications, 1990.

McCarthy, Flor, S.D.B. *And the Master Answered....*Notre Dame, IN: Ave Maria Press, 1985.

McKenna, Megan, and Tony Cowan. *Keepers of the Story.* Maryknoll, NY: Orbis Books, 1997.

Mellon, Nancy. *Storytelling and the Art of Imagination.* Rockport, NY: Element, Inc., 1992.

Meyer, Gabriel. *In the Shade of the Terebinth: Tales of a Night Journey.* Leavenworth, KS: Forest of Peace Publishing, 1994.

Miller, Donald. *The Gospel and Mother Goose.* Elgin, IL: Brethren Press, 1987.

Minghella, Anthony, ed. *Jim Henson's The Storyteller.* NY: Borzoi-Alfred A. Knopf, Inc., 1991.

National Storytelling Association. *Tales as Tools: The Power of Story in the Classroom.* Jonesborough, TN: The National Storytelling Press, 1994.

————. *Many Voices: True Tales from America's Past.* Jonesborough, TN: The National Storytelling Press, 1995.

Nelson, Pat. *Magic Minutes.* Englewood, CO: Libraries Unlimited, Inc., 1993.

Newcombe, Jack. *A Christmas Treasury.* NY: Viking Press, 1982.

Newman, Louis I. *The Hasidic Anthology: Tales and Teachings of the Hasidim.* NY: Schocken Books, 1963 (4th printing, 1975).

*The Night the Stars Sang: The Wonder That Is Christmas.* Tarrytown, NY: Gleneida Publishing Group-Triumph

Books, 1991 (by special arrangement with Guidepost Books).

Nomura, Yushi. *Desert Wisdom: Sayings from the Desert Fathers.* New York: Image Books, 1984.

O'Connor, Ulick. *Irish Tales and Sagas.* London: Dragon Books, 1985.

O'Faolain, Eileen. *Irish Sagas and Folk Tales.* NY: Avenel Books, 1982.

Olszewski, Daryl. *Balloons! Candy! Toys! and Other Parables for Storytellers.* San Jose, CA: Resource Publications, 1986.

Parry Jones, D., ed. *Welsh Legends and Fairy Lore.* NY: Barnes and Noble-Marboro Books by arrangement with B. T. Batsford, Ltd., 1992.

Paulus, Trina. *Hope for the Flowers.* Mahwah, NJ: Paulist Press, 1972.

Pellowski, Anne. *The World of Storytelling.* Revised edition. NY: H. W. Wilson, 1990.

Polsky, Howard W, and Yaella Wozner. *Everyday Miracles: The Healing Wisdom of Hasidic Stories.* Northvale, NJ: Jason Aronson Inc., 1989.

Powers, C. P., Isaias. *Nameless Faces in the Life of Jesus.* Mystic, CT: Twenty-Third Publications, 1981.

———. *Father Ike's Stories for Children.* Mystic, CT: Twenty-Third Publications, 1988.

Prather, Hugh, and Gayle Prather. *Parables from Other Planets.* NY: Bantam Books, 1991.

Pu, Songling. *Strange Tales from Make-Do Studio.* Beijing: Foreign Language Press, 1989.

Ramanujan, A. K., ed. *Folktales from India.* NY: Pantheon Books-Random House, 1991.

Rideau, S. Noel. *Uncle Noel's Fun Fables.* Covington, LA: Aesop Systems Publishing Co., 1991.

———. *Teacher's Guide for Uncle Noel's Fun Fables.* Covington, LA: Aesop Systems Publishing Co., 1991.

Robbennolt, Roger. *Tales of Tony Great Turtle*. Leavenworth, KS: Forest of Peace Publishing, 1994.

Schwartz, Howard, and Barbara Rush, eds. *The Diamond Tree: Jewish Tales from Around the World*. NY: Harper-Collins, 1991.

Seuss, Dr. *Oh, the Places You'll Go!* NY: Random House, 1990.

Shah, Idries. *The Hundred Tales of Wisdom*. London: Octagon Press, 1978.

————. *The Subtleties of the Inimitable Mulla Nasrudin* and *The Exploits of the Incomparable Mulla Nasrudin: Two Volumes in One*. London: Octagon Press, 1983.

————. *Seeker After Truth*. London: Octagon Press, 1982, 1992.

————. *World Tales*. London: Octagon Press, 1991.

————. *Tales of the Dervishes: Teaching Stories of the Sufi Masters over the Past Thousand Years*. 1967. NY: Penguin-ARKANA, 1993.

Shedlock, Marie L. *The Art of the Story Teller*. 3rd ed. NY: Dover Publications, 1951.

*Short Tales of the Ming and Qing*. Beijing: Panda Books-Chinese Literature Press, 1996.

Simpkinson, Charles, and Anne Simpkinson, eds. *Sacred Stories: A Celebration of the Power of Stories to Transform and Heal*. San Francisco: HarperSanFrancisco, 1993.

Singer, Isaac Bashevis. *Stories for Children*. NY: Farrar, Straus and Giroux, 1984.

————. *The Image and Other Stories*. London: Jonathan Cape, Ltd., 1985.

Smith, Richard Gordon. *Ancient Tales and Folklore of Japan*. London: Bracken Books, 1986.

Stanton, Sue. *Boston and the Feast of St. Francis*. Mahwah, NJ: Paulist Press, 1994.

Stoddard, Sandol. *The Rules and Mysteries of Brother Solomon*. Mahwah, NJ: Paulist Press, 1987.

Stone, Richard. *The Healing Art of Storytelling.* NY: Hyperion, 1996.

Stromberg, Bob. *Why Geese Fly Farther Than Eagles.* Colorado Springs: Focus on the Family Publications, 1992.

Sutherland, Zena, and Myra Cohn Liningston, eds. *The Scott, Foresman Anthology of Children's Literature.* IL: Scott, Foresman and Co., 1984.

Tazewell, Charles. *The Littlest Angel.* Nashville: Ideals Publishing, 1946.

Theophane the Monk. *Tales of a Magic Monastery.* NY: Crossroad, 1981.

Thoma, Clemens, and Michael Wyschogrod, eds. *Parable and Story in Judaism and Christianity.* Mahwah, NJ: Paulist Press, 1989.

Thompson, Stith. *The Folktale.* Los Angeles: The University of California Press, 1977.

Valles, Carlos G., S.J. *Tales of the City of God.* Chicago: Loyola University Press, 1993.

Van Dyke, Henry, and James S. Bell, eds. *A Treasury of Christmas Stories.* Wheaton, IL: Harold Shaw Publishers, 1993.

Vecsey, Christopher. *Imagine Ourselves Richly: Mythic Narratives of North American Indians.* San Francisco: HarperCollins, 1991.

Walker, Scott. *Glimpses of God: Stories That Point the Way.* Minneapolis, MN: Augsburg Fortress, 1997.

Ward, Benedicta, trans. *The Sayings of the Desert Fathers.* Kalamazoo, MI: Cistercian Publications, 1975 (revised 1984).

Weinreich, Beatrice Silverman, ed. *Yiddish Folktales.* Translated by Leonard Wolf. NY: Pantheon-Random House, 1988.

Werner, E. T. C. *Myths and Legends of China.* Mineola, NY: Dover Publications, 1994.

Wharton, Paul, ed. *Stories and Parables for Preachers and Teachers.* NY: Paulist Press, 1986.

White, William R., ed. *Speaking in Stories*. Minneapolis: Augsburg, 1982.

———. *Stories for Telling*. Minneapolis: Augsburg, 1986.

———. *Stories for the Journey*. Minneapolis: Augsburg, 1988.

———. *Stories for the Gathering*. Minneapolis: Augsburg, 1997.

Wiesel, Elie. *Souls on Fire: Portraits and Legends of Hasidic Masters*. NY: Summit Books, 1972.

———. *Somewhere a Master: Further Hasidic Portraits and Legends*. NY: Summit Books, 1981.

Wilde, Oscar. *The Happy Prince and Other Fairy Tales*. NY: Dover, 1992.

———. *The Fairy Tales of Oscar Wilde*. NY: Henry Holt and Co., 1993.

Wood, Douglas. *Old Turtle*. Duluth, MN: Pfeifer-Hamilton Publishers, 1992.

Wrede, Patricia A. *Book of Enhancements*. NY: Jane Yolen Books/Harcourt Brace, 1996.

Yolen, Jane, ed. *Favorite Folktales from Around the World*. NY: Pantheon Books-Random House, 1986.

Zipes, Jack, ed. *Spells of Enchantment: The Wondrous Fairy Tales of Western Culture*. NY: Viking-Penguin, 1991.

———. *Aesop's Fables...and 200 other famous fables*. NY: Signet Classic-Penguin, 1992.

# Theme Index

| Theme: | Story Numbers: |
| --- | --- |
| Goals | 10, 49, 76 |
| God's Will | 27, 35 |
| "Golden Rule" | 12, 19, 22, 39, 40, 47, 48, 50, 51, 55, 59, 60, 67, 90, 94, 100 |
| Good Samaritan | 19, 22 |
| Gospel Witness | 35, 42, 47, 60, 69 |
| Grandparents | 19, 25 |
| Gratitude | 12, 22, 25, 73, 76 |
| Greed | 75, 84 |
| | |
| Habits, Bad | 38, 63 |
| Happiness | 12, 24, 41, 66, 71, 73, 98 |
| Healing | 20, 33 |
| Hiroshima/Nagasaki | 26 |
| Holiness | 24, 100 |
| Holy Family | 11, 16, 23, 24 |
| Holy Week | 33, 93 |
| Hope | 1, 3, 6, 18, 21, 27, 42, 44, 46, 53, 61, 62, 64 |
| Hospitality | 5, 13, 22, 39, 60, 65, 79, 94 |
| Humility | 25, 44, 53, 89 |
| Humor | 14, 12, 16, 24, 55, 56, 57, 74, 84, 87, 89 |
| Husband/Wife | 4, 70, 71, 73 |
| | |
| Influence, Positive | 16, 18, 60, 96 |
| Integrity | 37, 63, 81, 95 |
| Irish Blessing | 72 |
| | |
| Joy | 84 |
| Judgment | 30, 50 |
| | |
| Kindness | 12, 22, 39, 40, 51, 73, 90 |
| King, Martin L., Jr. | 50 |

| Theme: | Story Numbers: |
|---|---|
| Kipling, Rudyard | 85 |
| Labor Day | 20, 35, 81, 95 |
| Laity | 35, 60, 100 |
| Leadership | 7, 8, 21, 30, 37, 47, 88, 96 |
| Leadership, Servant | 35, 41 |
| Lent | 13, 15, 33, 48, 53, 56, 63, 67, 82, 83, 86, 93, 96 |
| Life Journey | 3, 7, 15, 19, 28, 29, 30, 31, 34, 41, 45, 46, 50, 54, 62, 66, 76, 85, 87, 88, 92, 94, 98, 99 |
| Light/Dark | 2, 42, 62, 65, 79 |
| Listening | 5, 28, 78, 91, 97 |
| Loneliness | 59 |
| Look/Find | 17, 21, 54, 66 |
| Love | 6, 11, 28, 32, 51, 58, 72, 64, 86 |
| Marriage | 58, 70, ,71, 72, 73 |
| Maturity | 2, 87 |
| Meaning/Purpose | 3, 45, 80 |
| Mediocrity | 55, 68 |
| Mentors | 19, 76, 100 |
| Mercy | 67 |
| Mercy Sunday | 33 |
| Mercy, Works of | 1, 5, 22, 39, 47, 48, 59, 60, 62, 79, 90, 94 |
| Michelangelo | 95 |
| Middle Age | 34 |
| Ministry | 35, 41, 60 |
| Mother/Daughter | 17, 34, 66, 74 |
| Mother-in-Law | 25 |
| Mothers | 6, 80, 98 |

| Theme: | Story Numbers: |
| --- | --- |
| Respect | 11, 73, 91 |
| Responsibility | 88, 96, 98 |
| Resurrection | 53 |
| Role Model | 8, 22, 28, 42, 97 |
| | |
| Sacrament of the Sick | 29 |
| Sacrifice | 48, 64 |
| Saints | 42 |
| School | 10 |
| Self-Esteem | 16, 17, 54, 59 |
| Sermon on the Mount | 50, 60, 67, 83 |
| Service | 1, 41, 47 58, 59, 83, 94 |
| Sin | 15, 33, 63, 82, 84 |
| Social Justice | 26, 50, 83 |
| Sow/Reap | 11, 12, 21, 41, 55, 84, 96 |
| Spiritual Direction | 87, 100 |
| Spirituality | 5, 29, 41, 44, 57, 62, 76, 79, 80, 94, 100 |
| Spirituality of Work | 35 |
| Sports | 19, 49, 53, 57, 77 |
| St. Joseph | 35, 52, 81, 95 |
| St. Luke | 20 |
| Stress | 4, 74 |
| Success | 7, 10, 18, 44, 49 |
| Support | 8, 77, 82 |
| Synergy | 88, 99 |
| | |
| Teaching | 1, 19, 21, 43, 45, 46, 57 |
| Teamwork | 77, 82, 88, 99 |
| Teenagers | 3, 18, 21, 36, 43, 45, 46, 48, 59, 68, 75, 85, 87, 91, 92 |
| Thanksgiving | 12, 39, 84 |
| Transformation | 36 |
| Trust | 32 |

| Theme: | Story Numbers: |
|---|---|
| Understanding | 24, 28, 30, 32, 36, 40, 45, 76, 78, 91 |
| Vengeance | 93 |
| Virtue | 47, 81, 84 |
| Vocation | 100 |
| Volunteers | 59, 94 |
| War | 26 |
| Wealth | 75 |
| Wedding | 71, 72 |
| Wilson, Woodrow | 7 |
| Wisdom | 6, 10, 15, 30, 32, 40, 45, 71, 76, 92, 98 |
| Worry | 4, 54, 61, 92 |
| Youth | 46, 98 |
| Youth Ministry | 1, 3, 7, 8, 18, 37, 45, 46, 47, 49, 53, 57, 59, 63, 66, 85, 87, 91, 96, 99 |